SPEAKING PASCAL

SPEAKING PASCAL

Kenneth A. Bowen
Syracuse University

HAYDEN BOOK COMPANY, INC.
Rochelle Park, New Jersey

*For Alexandra
and Melissa*

Library of Congress Cataloging in Publication Data

Bowen, Kenneth A.
  Speaking Pascal.

  Bibliography: p.
  Includes index.
  1. PASCAL (Computer program language) I. Title.
QA76.73.P2B66   001.64'24   81-5390
ISBN 0-8104-5164-6   AACR2

Printed in the United States of America

1	2	3	4	5	6	7	8	9	PRINTING

81	82	83	84	85	86	87	88	89	YEAR

Preface

Learning to program should be fun! This book makes learning to program in the language Pascal a pleasant experience. It is designed for beginners with no previous programming experience. The pace and approach are slow and careful, yet light-hearted and enjoyable. There are many carefully chosen examples which are used to motivate and illustrate the important ideas. These examples are chosen to reflect concerns from everyday life, such as diagnosing and treating winter colds, or choosing breakfast from a menu. Thus they are immediately meaningful and interesting to everyone. In this way, learning the fundamental ideas of Pascal becomes a pleasant task.

While presenting the elements of the particular programming language Pascal, I have tried to convey an understanding and appreciation of the top-down, structured approach to program design and construction. All of the principal examples are carefully developed with these methods. Experience has shown this approach to be the most reliable method of producing correct and understandable programs.

The version of Pascal presented is extremely close to the international standard for Pascal, and thus is widely available on many computers. The few deviations from the proposed standard are noted in the text. The version presented covers all the important constructs used in everyday programming. These are widely available on every computer which supports Pascal at all, and include procedures and functions, arrays, records, enumeration types, iteration and control, and input-output. A few constructs which are not widely used in everyday programming have been omitted.

This book has grown out of my experiences teaching Pascal and other programming languages at Syracuse University. To my colleagues at the School of Computer and Information Science I am indebted for many fruitful conversations over the years, and in particular to Lockwood Morris, with whom I first learned Pascal as we jointly taught the first course in this language at Syracuse.

To Henry Ledgard, I owe a very special thanks. As my editor, he has been both a wonderful source of ideas and a vigilant critic. In particular, he suggested that I transfer the top-down approach to the design and execution of the book itself, and was a great aid in actually accomplishing this. The contribution of Randall Bond, fine arts librarian at Syracuse, is immediately evident: he led me to the sources of the lovely illustrations in the text. Betsy Clarke helped with both the typing and final production – to her, many thanks.

And last, but far from least, I owe tremendous gratitude to my wife and daughters for their support and forbearance during the writing of this book.

Kenneth A. Bowen
Syracuse, New York
April, 1981

Contents

SPEAKING PASCAL

Chapter One

Talking to Computers: Introduction

     In the 35 odd years of their existence, electronic computers have undergone a remarkable growth and development that still continues today. The early legendary machines such as the ENIAC, the IAS computer, and the UNIVAC I were behemoth arrays of thousands of vacuum tubes that occupied large rooms, constantly broke down, and cost hundreds of thousands of dollars. Today far more powerful machines built out of miniaturized transistors occupy no more space than a typewriter, run reliably for years, and can be bought for less than $1,000 at retail stores throughout the United States. Despite this dramatic development, these modern machines are conceptually quite similar to their early counterparts. Both are sophisticated machines for manipulating electronic representations of data at incredibly high speeds. And both must be told explicitly what to do in these manipulations.

Popular myths to the contrary, computers themselves are not at all intelligent. They can no more think through solutions of problems on their own than a semi-trailer truck is capable of driving itself from New York to Los Angeles. In both cases, intelligent human guidance is needed. In the case of the semi-trailer truck, the human operator is always present, directing the actions of the truck at each moment. In the case of the computer, the human operator generally prepares a set of instructions (a program) for the machine in advance, and the computer follows these instructions as it goes about the manipulations to compute a solution to the problem at hand. In each case the intelligence is human; the expenditure of effort is mechanical or electronic.

The actual instructions that a computer is prepared to accept and execute are extremely primitive. Consequently the preparation of programs using these actual machine instructions is not only tedious and difficult, but also highly error-prone. This difficulty has led to the development of methods for controlling computers which use instructions that are more suitable for human use. These methods are generally termed *higher-order lanaguages* for computer programming.

The number and diversity of these languages is bewildering. A fragmentary list of some of the better-known languages includes ALGOL, APL, BASIC, COBOL, FORTRAN, JOVIAL, LISP, LOGO, Pascal, PL/I, PROLOG, SAIL, and SNOBOL. These various programming languages have been designed with differing goals. Some are intended to be general-purpose, while others are intended to be more suitable for business data processing, scientific numerical calculation, research in artificial intelligence, text processing, and so forth. In this book we will study the programming language Pascal. This is a modern, general-purpose programming language. Its design has benefited from experiences with earlier programming languages and is oriented towards so-called *structured programming* methods. At the present time Pascal is regarded as a paradigm among programming languages. As such, it has become widely available on most computers.

1.1   A Program to Read Aloud

One of the intents of the designer of Pascal (Nicklaus Wirth) was to produce a computer language that was easy to learn. He succeeded at this, and one of the consequences of his success is that Pascal makes possible the writing of programs that are clear and easy to understand. To illustrate his success in doing this, consider Program 1-1. Its purpose is to set up a small dialogue between the computer and the user at the terminal. The computer will ask the user for the time of

```
program TIMEOFDAY(INPUT,OUTPUT);                                        1
(* ------------------------------------------------------------- *    2
 *       This program accepts as input a so-called military      *    3
 * time specification, such as 0745 or 2130, and outputs the     *    4
 * corresponding time in the usual am/pm format.                 *    5
 * ------------------------------------------------------------- *)   6
                                                                        7
    var                                                                 8
       MILTIME, HOURS, MINS: INTEGER;                                   9
                                                                       10
begin                                                                  11
                                                                       12
    WRITE('Please type the time in military format: ');                13
    READ(MILTIME);                                                     14
                                                                       15
    HOURS := MILTIME div 100;                                          16
    MINS  := MILTIME mod 100;                                          17
                                                                       18
    WRITE('The time at the tone is: ');                                19
                                                                       20
    if (HOURS = 0) and (MINS = 0) then                                 21
       WRITE(' MIDNIGHT')                                              22
    else if HOURS < 1 then                                             23
       WRITE('12:, MINS, 'a.m.')                                       24
    else if HOURS < 12 then                                            25
       WRITE(HOURS, ':', MINS, 'a.m.')                                 26
    else if (HOURS = 12) and (MINS = 0) then                           27
       WRITE(' NOON')                                                  28
    else if (HOURS = 12) and (MINS > 0) then                           29
       WRITE(HOURS, ':', MINS, 'p.m.')                                 30
    else                                                               31
       WRITE((HOURS - 12), ':', MINS, 'p.m.');                         32
                                                                       33
end.                                                                   34
```

Program 1-1 A Simple Program to Compute the Time of Day.

day expressed in the 24-hour or "military" format. The user supplies it, and the computer responds with the time expressed in the common a.m./p.m. format.

Though we have not yet studied the details of Pascal, it is possible to read this program (aloud) and follow its operation.

The first line simply identifies the start of the program. The next five lines, from the opening (* to the closing *) are a comment, which has no effect on the machine but simply describes the action of the program for the benefit of human readers. Then in lines 8 and 9 there occurs a *variable declaration*. This simply asserts that we intend to use the words MILTIME, HOURS, MINS as names of "containers" or variables for holding integers. The action part of the program starts in line 11. (Line numbers are present in this program for reference only. Normally Pascal programs do not contain line numbers.)

The first action is to write out the following message on the terminal:

Please type the time in military format

The next action (in line 14) is to read in the integer typed on the terminal by the user and store it in the variable or container called MILTIME. Then the hours in this military time are obtained by dividing the value of MILTIME by 100 and obtaining the integer quotient. The result is stored in the variable HOURS. The remaining minutes in MILTIME are obtained (in line 17) as the remainder when the value in MILTIME is divided by 100. This result is stored in the variable MINS. Next the message

The time at the tone is

is printed out on the terminal (and no new line is started).

Finally, beginning at line 21, the program must make a decision as to what to print out for the time. It proceeds as follows:

1. If both HOURS and MINS contain value 0, the time must be midnight, and so it prints this.

2. However, if either the value in HOURS is not 0 or the value in MINS is not 0, but the value in HOURS is less than 12, it must be morning; and so the program prints out the value in HOURS followed by a colon (:), in turn followed by the value in MINS, and finally the expression 'a.m.'.

3. Now, if the value in HOURS is precisely 12 and the value in MINS is 0, it must be noon and the program prints this.

4. But if the value in HOURS is still 12 and the value in MINS is not 0, it must be between noon and 1 p.m.; and so the

program prints out 12 followed by a colon followed by the value in MINS, which is finally followed by the expression 'p.m.'.

5. In the final case, the value in HOURS must be greater than 12. Therefore, we must correct it by subtracting 12 from it. The program does this as it prints out the time.

Notice how much English it took to explicate the simple Pascal text for this decision. Yet the English is no clearer! We will find this quite often to be true: if we know precisely what we wish to do, it is often easier to say it in Pascal than in English.

1.2 Your Conversational Partner

Just as it is possible to operate a car or truck with no knowledge of its inner mechanical workings, it is possible to program and operate computers with no knowledge of their inner electronic workings. But a vehicle can be driven more effectively and efficiently if one possesses some knowledge of its inner design. Moreover, this knowledge becomes even more valuable in dealing with the inevitable minor malfunctions and difficulties that can arise during a trip.

The same is true for computers. The person who has some knowledge of the inner construction of computers can design more efficient and effective programs, as well as deal more effectively with the problems ("bugs") which seem to inevitably arise in programming. This knowledge need not be at the level of the engineering and physical details of the machine's function, but rather at the logical or conceptual level.

Viewed quite simplistically, a computer can be seen as a device that accepts certain data as input and gives forth other data as output, as indicated in Figure 1-1.

INPUT ⟶ COMPUTER ⟶ OUTPUT

Figure 1-1. The Computer as a Black Box.

However, to use the machine effectively, we will need to look inside it a bit. If we begin breaking down the logical structure of a computer, we discover that it has the following requirements:

- There must be devices for inputting both data and instructions to the machine and for outputting the results of its computations. These are collectively known as input-output devices, or I-O for short.

- There must be a *central processor* that interprets the instructions and carries out the arithmetic and logical computations.

- There must be a *memory* in which both data and instructions can be stored and retrieved by the central processor.

Our diagram of the computer might now appear as in Figure 1-2.

Figure 1-2.   Elementary Computer Structure.

To fully grasp some of what follows, we will need to break this diagram down a bit further. First we note that there exist a variety of input-output devices, some of which can do both input and output, and others that are strictly limited to one function or the other. Both the teletype (which for our purposes includes Decwriters, IBM 2741 terminals, and so forth) and the graphics display terminal, as well as punched paper tape, can do both input and output. On the other hand, the card reader can only input data, while the card punch, high-speed line printer, and plotter can only output data.

Computers also have several types of memory. The fastest memory, in the sense that data can be entered into it and recopied from it faster than in any other type, is known as *primary storage* memory. This is the memory unit used directly by the central processor. (It is sometimes called *core* memory, reflecting the fact that in many of the early large-scale machines this memory was made up of many small magnetic iron "cores.") Unfortunately, primary memory units are very expensive and tend to be bulky relative to the amount of information they can store. Hence large-scale machines make use of several other slower, but more economical and compact, memory units. The first of these is the *magnetic disk*, which is the fastest memory after primary memory. These disks resemble large phonograph records that have been coated on both sides with a brown magnetic substance similar to that used on ordinary magnetic tape. Next in order of memory speed comes magnetic tape itself. And last of all is the ubiquitous punched card. Recently, magnetic tape in the form of cassettes has also come into use, especially with smaller computer systems.

Our logical diagram of a large computer might now appear as in Figure 1-3.

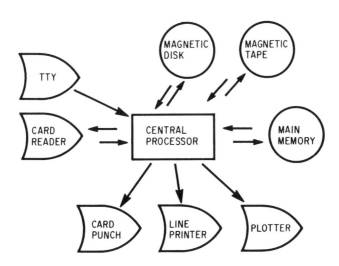

Figure 1-3. Logical Structure of a Computer.

The input-output devices indicated simply form the basic comple-ment for a general-purpose installation. In special-purpose installations, sensors and control motors are added. By means of these additions, computers can be used to monitor and control industrial and manufacturing processes, direct environmental control in buildings and homes, and run games and toys.

As we indicated, in such a computer we store not only numbers and other data in the memory but also the instructions for a computation. Thus the machine is able to obtain and read its instructions just as fast as it can obtain its data. The question obviously arises as to what form we can imagine the data and instructions to take when they are stored in memory. Are they represented in a form resembling our ordinary ways of writing or in some other manner? Unfortunately for the beginning student, the form in which they appear in memory is quite different from our ordinary representations. In fact, one can say that all of the items − numbers, other data, and instructions − are represented in a language whose only symbols are the digits 0 and 1. This apparently bizarre state of affairs is caused by engineering limitations in the construction of computers. Needless to say, programming in "machine language" is tedious in the extreme.

The central processing unit has capabilities for manipulating the words of this machine language. Among some of its capabilities are the following:

- Comparing two words to see if they are equal.

- Taking two words that represent numbers and adding, subtracting, multiplying, or dividing them to produce the word representing the sum, difference, product, or quotient, respectively.

- Taking a word representing a letter or digit and causing the letter or digit to be output, say on a teletype.

- Sensing that a key has been typed on a teletype, and obtaining the word representing the character on the key.

These capabilities are really quite primitive. The power of computers arises from their ability to perform such operations over and over at incredibly high speeds (thousands or millions of operations per second). High-level languages such as Pascal provide the capability to control such runaway speed and power without the tedium and difficulty of machine-language programming.

1.3   Behind the Conversation

When the statements of a higher level programming language such as Pascal are typed in or read in from the punched card reader, they are automatically coded into a form that the machine can manipulate.

Though the higher level statements are in a binary code, the coded form usually is not in the form of a machine-language instruction; often, from the computer's point of view, the coded form is just gibberish. So the second stage of the translation procedure involves the translation of these coded statements into instructions intelligible by the machine. This second stage translation is not physically built into the machine, but is accomplished by a complex program called an interpreter or compiler. Each higher level programming language has its own interpreter, compiler, or both.

The difference between an interpreter and a compiler lies in their approach to the translation of the statements of the higher order language. Roughly, an interpreter reads each individual statement or command of the program and immediately translates and executes it, while a compiler translates the entire program before actual execution begins. There are advantages and disadvantages to each approach. In general, once a compiler has finished the total translation of a program, the actual execution speed of this *compiled* program is faster than that of the same original (*source*) program executed by an interpreter. Moreover, the amount of memory occupied by the compiled program is much less than the combined space occupied by the source program together with the interpreter program. Since main memory is a scarce and expensive commodity, this is a serious consideration. On the other hand, compilers as programs themselves are usually much larger and more complex than interpreter programs; they can be so big as to be impossible to fit in the memory of a microcomputer. Moreover, when the source program contains errors (*bugs*), it is often much easier to diagnose these errors with the assistance of an interpreter than with a compiler.

You will recall that an interpreter or a compiler for a higher level language is itself just a computer program. This program, which *is* the interpreter or compiler, is called an *implementation* of the higher level language. Since it is usually a program for a particular kind of computer, it is called an implementation of the higher level language *on* that computer. For example, one speaks of implementations of Pascal on IBM 370 computers, on CDC 6600 computers, and so forth.

Some languages (such as LISP) are implemented using both compilers and interpreters. Some (such as BASIC and LOGO) primarily use interpreters, and others (including Pascal) primarily use compilers. Pascal has been implemented on most mainframe and minicomputers available today, as well as on a wide range of microcomputers. All of these implementations differ in one degree or another. The fine details of these differences are usually not of concern and can be determined by consulting the appropriate computer's manuals.

What can we expect from a programming language? Fundamentally it should provide us with two things. First, it must provide the means to represent the objects about which we must compute, be they numbers, words, sentences, accounts receivable, airline network schedules, and so on. And second, it must provide us with the means of expressing the actions necessary to carry out our intended computations.

Put another way, a programming language must supply data structures appropriate to our problems and must also provide us with the means for describing the *algorithms* we formulate for manipulating these structures in order to solve our problems. For example, if we are interested in creating a program to aid travel agents in scheduling airline trips, our programming language must provide data structures for conveniently representing the complex consisting of cities and the scheduled flights between them, and must also provide us with the means to express algorithms for exploring this complex to determine the most convenient combination of flights for getting a traveler to her or his destination.

General-purpose programming languages such as Pascal meet these requirements in the following ways. First, they directly provide representations of widely used computational objects such as integers, real numbers, characters, and truth-values (true, false); these are regarded as primitive objects. Then they provide methods of building more complex data representations out of simpler ones by means of such operations as forming lists, arrays, and sets of previously constructed objects. With regard to the expression of algorithms, they provide primitive functions such as addition for manipulating the primitive data representations. And then they provide the means for defining more complex operations on both the primitive and non-primitive data structures using such operations as composition of functions, iteration of previously defined operations, testing the truth or falsity of a predicate and carrying out different operations according to the results of that test, and so on.

The chapters that follow elaborate these ideas, as they are realized in the language Pascal, and illustrate their use with a variety of programming problems.

Chapter Two

Money Talk: Integer Expressions

Everyone uses ordinary whole numbers (*integers*) throughout daily life. We express temperatures (89 degrees), addresses (7856 von Neumann Drive), and salaries ($10,000 per year), among many other things, using whole numbers. In fact, we use positive and negative forms: 5 degrees below zero, $1,500 in the red, and so forth. Because of this ubiquity, any computer language worth its salt (which does include Pascal) must provide means for talking about integers. And so, we will begin our first conversations in Pascal by talking about integers. In this chapter, we will discuss the following topics:

- Communicating with a computer.
- Organizing simple Pascal programs.
- Expressing integers in Pascal.
- Getting the machine to read data and print results.
- Using operations like addition and subtraction.
- Using variables for integers in Pascal.
- Organizing and documenting your work.

2.1   Striking Up a Conversation

Computers come in an incredible array of sizes, shapes, and dispositions. Though Pascal is intended to be uniform from machine to machine, your means of direct communication with various machines may vary widely. You may be able to work in a "conversational" mode with your machine, typing in commands and getting an immediate response, or you may have to work in a "batch" mode whereby you punch cards with your commands, submit the collection (*deck*) of cards for reading into the machine, and collect some printed output later. Let us hope that you can communicate with your computer in the conversational mode! This certainly is the style for almost all micro- and minicomputers and for a large number of mainframes. We will assume throughout this book that this is in fact your mode of communication. Everything we say about Pascal is true for the batch style of computing, but some of the "conversations" we will be constructing would become very stilted in the batch environment.

So presumably you have a terminal device to communicate with your computer. It may be a CRT (TV-screen type) or it may be typewriter-like. Either way, when you turn it on you have begun to establish communication with the computer's *monitor* or *operating system*. This is just another program (always running) that is designed to make it easier for you to utilize the machine. If you are working on a small microcomputer, chances are you are its only user and it awaits your command the moment you turn it on. If you are using a somewhat larger minicomputer or a mainframe, in all likelihood you are *time-sharing* the computer with other users. In this case, you must usually identify yourself as a bona fide user via the system's *sign-on* procedure. These procedures vary from machine to machine, and so we leave it to you to learn the details of the process.

In any event, you should soon find yourself with the operating system awaiting your wish. And what is that? To converse in Pascal, of course! Here we arrive at the first shock: the operating system is not prepared to talk Pascal! While this situation reflects poorly on the literacy of the operating system, it is prepared to put us in contact with someone who does speak Pascal, namely the Pascal compiler.

But then comes the second shock: the Pascal compiler is not prepared to accept one sentence at a time from you and respond to each individually, as one would expect in almost any human conversation. Instead, the Pascal compiler is prepared to accept a small speech from you (that is, a program) and to respond to you concerning its views on the soundness of what you have said. If it feels that you have uttered something approaching nonsense, it will usually (politely) inform you of this. And if it feels that what you have uttered at least appears sensible on the surface, it will translate your speech into a set of machine instructions that will cause the machine to do your bidding. And, as we shall see, these instructions can have the effect of causing small dialogues between you and your machine.

(Occasionally, people are offended by speaking of the machine in "human" terms. Yet the intent of high-level machine languages is really to lead us to just that mode. We really don't want to know the details of the machine's functioning. Instead, we want to focus on the problem we have to solve and to express the directions for finding the solution in a clear and precise shorthand much as we would to a poorly educated, literal-minded human assistant. Pascal provides us with such a linguistic tool, and so we will occasionally allow ourselves the latitude of such talk.)

Now there remains the problem of composing and conveying your speech to the Pascal compiler. For this you will make use of one of probably several *editors* available on your computer. This is yet another program designed to make life easier for you. It performs such functions as allowing you to type in your text and to make changes and corrections. Like computers themselves, editors vary tremendously, and so we will not attempt to discuss the details of their use. Rather, you must consult the documentation for your computer on the use of its editors. You really need only learn very little:

- How to type in lines of program text.

- How to correct or replace previously typed in lines.

Usually one gives names to such program speeches. These names are then used when discussing the speech with the operating system or the Pascal compiler. When your speech is typed in and named (say with the name MYPROGRAM), you must indicate to the operating system that you want to send it to the Pascal compiler (in jargon, to have it *compiled*). Typically you issue a command such as

```
RUN MYPROGRAM
```

or

```
COMPILE MYPROGRAM
```

The Pascal compiler will then identify itself in some way or other, and give you messages concerning your program.

Hopefully, the substance of these messages will be that your program appears sensible, that it has been translated, and that you can have the machine execute the translated version. (In jargon you are almost certain to encounter, the original Pascal program is called the *source* program, and the translation of it into machine language is called the *object program* or *object module*.) If you are not so lucky, the Pascal compiler will give you a variety of messages on your errors in usage of Pascal. What constitutes correct and incorrect usage is of course what we will study in the course of this text. When you encounter such error messages, you should make use of the editor to change your program and correct these errors. Some are simply the result of typing mistakes. Others are caused by misconceptions about Pascal.

2.2   Your Response

Having dispensed with these pleasantries and generalities, let us get down to the business of learning to speak in Pascal. Since we are going to begin by speaking about numbers, we must know how to describe them. Fortunately, Pascal describes integers almost as we do in ordinary written discourse. All of the following are perfectly correct descriptions of integers:

       345   1776   1000000   −5   −2001

The only difference between these examples and the ordinary form is the lack of commas for grouping the digits. Thus, instead of writing 1,000,000 as we usually do, Pascal insists on writing 1000000.

Now that we can describe numbers, what can we say about them? Basically, we can make assertions about them, and we can command the machine to do things with them. The assertions we can make are those of comparison. Namely, we can compare two numbers to decide whether they are equal or unequal, or whether one is greater or less than the other. The acts we can command the machine to carry out include writing or typing on our terminal; adding, subtracting, and multiplying two integers; and finding the quotient and remainder of one on division by the other.

Let us start with the command to cause the machine to print the integer on the terminal. It is simply

       WRITE(1776)

This command will cause 1776 to be written on the output device; usually this is your terminal. It can be expanded to deal with any number of integers at once. For example, to cause 1, 0, and −1 to be printed, use

       WRITE(1, 0, −1)

The effect of this, when executed by the machine, would be

    1   0   −1

Any number of integers may be included in the command. Simply separate the individual elements of the list by commas. You may use additional spaces for legibility (as we did above), but they are not necessary: WRITE(1, 0, −1) would be understood and have the same effect.

To add and subtract integers, we use the ordinary notation. For instance,

    34 + 19   1776 + 200   −23 + 7

are all acceptable *integer expressions* in Pascal. In the appropriate contexts, they would each be evaluated, yielding 53, 1976, and −16, respectively. One appropriate context for them is in the WRITE statement. The statement

    WRITE(34 + 19)

will cause 53 to be written on the terminal, while

    WRITE(34 + 19, 1776 + 200, −23 + 7)

will cause

    53   1976   −16

to be printed on the terminal. As we noted in connection with the WRITE statement, spaces are useful, but not necessary, in integer expressions. Thus

    34+19   1776+200   −23+7

are also acceptable integer expressions. However, the judicious use of spaces in integer expressions (and much else) substantially improves the legibility of the program for its human readers. We strongly advocate their use.

Multiplication is indicated as usual, except that the symbol * is used instead of the usual cross. Thus 15 * 5 indicates the result of multiplying 15 by 5 (namely, 75). Complex integer expressions utilizing several operations are acceptable, as the following examples show:

    13 * (23 − 19)   (34 − (4 * (5 + 2))) * 7

As these examples indicate, parentheses may be used to group terms. On the other hand, parentheses may often be dropped. The common convention that multiplications and divisions are performed before additions and subtractions applies. Thus

13 * 23 - 19

would be understood as (13 * 23) - 19.

Finally, integer division is dealt with using the operators *div* and *mod*. The integer quotient of A by B is expressed as

A div B

Recall that the quotient of A by B is the largest integer Q so that Q * B ≤ A. If Q is the quotient of A by B, then the *remainder* on dividing A by B is A - (Q * B). In Pascal, the remainder is written as

A mod b

Thus if you are working with an amount originally in cents, say 243 cents, and you wish to express it in dollars and cents, then 243 *div* 100 is 2 (the number of dollars), and 243 *mod* 100 is 43 (the remaining number of cents.)

We now can compose our first complete Pascal program. Suppose that what we seek is the answer to the following calculation:

1776 mod 4 = ?

(Perhaps we want to know whether 1776 was a leap year.) A complete program to print the answer to this problem on the terminal is given in Program 2-1.

```
program CALCULATION(OUTPUT);
(* A simple integer calculation. *)
begin
    WRITE(1776 mod 4)
end.
```

Program 2-1. A Simple Calculation.

By examining this text, we can discover a number of important facts about the structure of Pascal programs. The first observation is that the program splits into two parts, called the *heading* and *body*.

The *heading* is everything from the beginning up to, but not including, the first occurrence of the word *begin*. The *body* is everything from that first *begin* to the last line. Thus in this example, the heading consists of the the first two lines, while the body consists of the last three:

```
program CALCULATION(OUTPUT);
(* A simple integer calculation. *)    } Heading
begin
    WRITE(1776 mod 4)                  } Body
end
```

The lowercase words in this program are called *reserved words*. (The fact that they are lowercase here is not what is important. That will be used simply to set them off from the rest of the text. They may in fact be upper or lower case.) In our small example, the reserved words occurring are: program, begin, end, mod. Altogether, Pascal has 35 reserved words. We will gradually encounter them as we proceed through the text. The reserved word *program* occurs at only one point in any Pascal program: the first line. It must be the first word of this line, and must be followed by a word (of the programmer's choosing) used to name the program, and this in turn must be followed by a semicolon. (Later we will discuss the other things that may also occur before the semicolon.) This word following *program* belongs to the class of *identifiers*. Besides their use to name the program itself, identifiers are used to name or identify a great many other entities in Pascal programs. An identifier is defined to be any sequence of letters and digits whose first character is a letter; moreover, it may *not* be one of Pascal's reserved words. Thus each of the following are identifiers:

```
PENNY   CHANGE   MINE   XY23G   TOTALCHANGE
```

On the other hand, the following fail to be identifiers:

```
23SKIDOO   MY#SCORE   $SALARY
```

The second line of the program is a *comment*. It will have no effect whatsover on the machine: the compiler ignores it entirely. Comments are added to programs to aid the human reader. Generally, any text occurring between { and }, or between (* and *) is a comment, and is thus ignored. Comments can appear anywhere in the program. In our example, the program is simple, so the comment too is simple.

The instructions the machine is to carry out appear in the body of the program. And the program itself is terminated by the full-stop or period following the final *end*.

Next suppose we wish to expand our program to perform a second calculation in addition to the first, say to print out the answer to:

    1984 mod 4 = ?

(We also want to know whether 1984 will be a leap year.) By now you know that the program statement which will do the trick is

    WRITE(1984 mod 4)

Thus we need only add this statement to the body of the program, as indicated in Program 2-2.

```
program CALCULATION(OUTPUT);
(* A small calculation *)
begin
  WRITE(1776 mod 4);
  WRITE(1984 mod 4)
end.
```

Program 2-2.   A Small Calculation.

Notice that the two WRITE statements in the body are separated by a semicolon. This is always true of adjacent statements in the body of a Pascal program: they are separated by semicolons.

The output of this program will appear:

        0   0

This may be just slightly surprising! Since there are two WRITE commands in the body of the program, shouldn't the two numbers occur on different lines? Obviously, the answer is that Pascal doesn't see things that way. Instead, when the WRITE statement is executed, the items requested are printed on the terminal, *and no new line is started*! Thus the next WRITE statement will begin writing where the last one left off. (Or, in our example, almost where the last one left off. Pascal always assumes that it should allot 12 spaces for printing integers. If the actual integer doesn't fill up 12 spaces, it pads the printing with extra blank spaces on the left. And if the integer takes more than 12 spaces, Pascal adds the necessary extra spaces.)

Fortunately, there is a way to get new lines started: use the command WRITELN instead of WRITE. The difference between the two is this. WRITELN behaves just like WRITE except that after it finishes printing the requested items, it starts a new line on the terminal. Then the next WRITE or WRITELN command will start printing at the beginning of the next line. Thus to get the output of our program on two separate lines, we modify our program as shown in Program 2-3.

```
program CALCULATION(OUTPUT);
(* A small calculation *)
begin
    WRITELN(1776 mod 4);
    WRITE(1984 mod 4)
end.
```

Program 2-3. A Small Calculation.

The output of this program is now

    0
    0

Each time a new line is to be started after some printing, a WRITELN must be used. So if there are many lines, there will be many WRITELN statements. Put another way, one can use WRITELN almost everywhere. You only need to use a plain WRITE statement whenever you are sure you do *not* want a new line started.

This sample program is so simple that we know the significance of these two numbers: the first is the answer to the first calculation, and so forth. However, the output of more complicated programs may be harder to decipher if the results are not labeled or identified in some way. Pascal provides facilities for this by allowing the presence of *strings* or *literals* in WRITE and WRITELN statements. A *string* is simply any sequence of characters enclosed within single quote signs. The following are examples of strings:

    'Answer to first calculation ='
    'Alexandra''s frog jumped!'

As the second example illustrates, if you wish to include a single quote sign itself as a character in the string, it must be typed twice at the point where it is to occur. Now we may modify our program to identify its output, as indicated in Program 2-4.

```
program CALCULATION(OUTPUT);
(* A small calculation *)
begin
    WRITELN('First answer =', 1776 mod 4);
    WRITE('Second answer =', 1984 mod 4)
end.
```

Program 2-4.   A Small Calculation.

The output of this program is:

    FIRST ANSWER =   0
    SECOND ANSWER =   0

One more point concerning output is worth considering at this moment. As you have seen, Pascal assumes that it should allow 12 spaces for printing integers; and if a given integer doesn't occupy the full 12 spaces, it pads it out with leading blanks. This is acceptable in some situations, but in others (such as preparing tables and reports) it may not be. So, what is needed is some method of controlling the assumed width that the integers must occupy on output. This, as you might expect by now, is controlled by additions to the WRITE and WRITELN statements. The width at which a given integer will be printed can be controlled by suffixing the integer with a colon (:)

followed by the number of spaces to be used. Thus

```
WRITE(23:2, 345:4)
```

will cause the integer 23 to be printed in precisely two spaces (and hence no extra padding), while 345 will be printed in four spaces (and hence padded with one leading space).

2.3   Program Structure

Up to this point, our Pascal programs have allowed us to use the computer as a very expensive (and cumbersome) calculator. One of the great powers of computing is the possibility of writing one program that can be used to calculate different outputs for a great variety of different inputs. Let us consider a simple version of such a problem. Suppose we wish to organize the following dialogue. The user at the terminal is asked to report the numbers of each type of coin he or she has at the moment. The user is to make this report by typing in the numbers at the terminal. Then the computer responds by reporting the total value of the change. Allowing ourselves to describe some of the actions in English, we can present the overall program to do this in Figure 2-1.

```
program CHANGE(INPUT,OUTPUT);
(*  --------------------------------------------------------------  *
 *        This program reads in six integer values, respectively  *
 *  representing the number of pennies, nickels, dimes, quarters,  *
 *  half-dollars, and silver dollars (Susan Bs) in coinage.       *
 *        The program outputs the total value of the coinage      *
 *  in dollars and cents.                                         *
 *  --------------------------------------------------------------  *)
begin
```

Obtain the numbers of each kind of coin;

Compute the total value in cents of the coinage;

Compute the number of dollars in this value;

Compute the total remaining cents in the value;

Output the results;

```
end.
```

Figure 2-1.   Outline of a Program to Count Change.

The very first action, to obtain the input, should start with a message to the user requesting the input. This we know how to do. For example:

```
WRITE('Numbers of coins =')
```

But to deal with the rest of the actions, we must introduce what is probably the single most powerful idea in all of science: the notion of a *variable*. This is best thought of as a conceptual "container" capable of taking on different values. Thus

the amount of my bank balance

is a conceptual container whose numeric value can fluctuate over time. Similarly,

the number of dimes in my pocket

and

the annual sales of microcomputers

are both conceptual containers whose values can change in time. In all of these examples, we identified *which* conceptual container we were concerned with by means of an English phrase.

Similarly, in Pascal we must be able to identify different variables with text of some sort. For this purpose, we use identifiers. Since identifiers can be used for a great many purposes in Pascal programs, we must describe or *declare* the use to which we will put a particular identifier. This is done by means of a *variable declaration*. This section occurs between the initial program line and the main body of the program. The section is set off by beginning with the reserved word *var*, after which follow the individual variable declarations. The individual integer variable declarations have the form:

identifier : integer

Thus to declare that the identifier NUMWIDGETS is to denote an individual variable, we write:

NUMWIDGETS : integer

If in addition the identifiers COSTPERWIDGET and TOTALCOST are also to be used as integer variables, we can add their declarations, separating them by semicolons (which are necessary):

NUMWIDGETS : integer;
COSTPERWIDGET : integer;
TOTALCOST : integer

Alternatively, we could combine the three declarations into one:

NUMWIDGETS,COSTPERWIDGET,TOTALCOST : integer

The reaction of the computer to such a declaration is to prepare a variable or container that is "the right size and shape" to hold integers and to associate the given identifier (for example, NUMWIDGETS) with this container. However, nothing is put into the container. (Of course: we haven't yet told it *what* we want to put into it.) Placing integers into a variable container is achieved by the *assignment statement*. The form of an integer assignment statement is:

variable := expression

The identifier associated with the *variable* must have been declared to be an integer variable in a variable declaration. The following are all acceptable assignment statements:

```
NUMWIDGETS := 23
COSTPERWIDGET := 5
TOTALCOST := NUMWIDGETS * COSTPERWIDGET
COSTPERWIDGET := 7
NUMWIDGETS := TOTALCOST div COSTPERWIDGET
```

The computer's action when executing an assignment statement is this: it first *evaluates* the expression on the right side of the assignment sign (:=) to obtain an integer value and then stores this value in the container associated with the identifier on the left-hand side of the sign. Thus the effect of the first assignment statement above is to store the integer 23 in the variable named NUMWIDGETS. If a variable appears in the integer expression on the right side, the value that is stored in it is used in the evaluation. However, the value in such a variable is not disturbed by this use. The computer simply "looks in" to see what the value is, and goes on about its business. Thus after executing the first three assignment statements, the value 23 is stored in the variable named NUMWIDGETS, the value 5 is stored in the variable COSTPERWIDGET, and the value 115 is stored in the variable named TOTALCOST.

Finally, if there already is an integer stored in the variable named by the identifier on the left-hand side of an assignment statement, this value is thrown away and replaced by the new value computed from the expression on the right side. Thus after executing the five assignment statements above in sequence, the variable COSTPERWIDGET will contain the integer 7, while the variables NUMWIDGETS and TOTALCOST will contain the integers 16 and 115, respectively.

The sequence of events is important. *First*, the right side is evaluated using whatever values are presently contained in the variables named in the expression, and *then* the computed value is stored in the variable named on the left side. Thus the same identifier can occur on *both* sides of the assignment sign, as in this example:

```
NUMWIDGETS := NUMWIDGETS + 7
```

Suppose now that the computer executes the following two statements in succession:

```
NUMWIDGETS := 23;
NUMWIDGETS := NUMWIDGETS + 7
```

This is what will happen: after the first statement is executed, the variable named NUMWIDGETS contains the value 23. When the computer sets out to execute the second statement, it begins by evaluating the right side first. Thus when it "peeks into" the variable named NUM-WIDGETS, it finds the value 23 and uses this in the evaluation, getting the result 30. It then throws away the current value in NUMWIDGETS (which is 23) and stores the result 30 in the variable NUMWIDGETS. Thus after the execution of these two assignment statements, the variable NUMWIDGETS contains the value 30.

Incorporating the need for variable declarations, our schematic program will now appear as given in Figure 2-2.

```
program CHANGE(INPUT,OUTPUT);
(*  ------------------------------------------------------------  *
 *        This program reads in six integar values, respectively  *
 *   representing the number of pennies, nickels, dimes, quarters, *
 *   half-dollars, and silver dollars (Susan Bs) in coinage.       *
 *        The program outputs the total value of the coinage       *
 *   in dollars and cents.                                         *
 *  ------------------------------------------------------------  *)
    var

        Declare the necessary variables here
begin

        Obtain the numbers of each type of coin;

        Compute the total value in cents of the coinage;

        Compute the total dollars in this value;

        Compute the total remaining cents in the value;

        Output the results;

end.
```

Figure 2-2.   Adding Variable Declarations to CHANGE.

Our problem now is to refine each of the English phrases into appropriate utterances in Pascal. Let us begin by considering the variables we will need. Certainly we will need one variable for each type of coin to store the number of that kind of coin the user possesses. It is sensible to use mnemonic names whenever possible. So why not use PENNIES, NICKELS, DIMES, QUARTERS, HALFDOLLARS, and DOLLARS as the names of the variables to hold the numbers of the associated coins? Next we will need one variable to contain the total value in cents of the coinage; let's use TOTALCHANGE for this. Finally, we need a variable for the number of dollars in the value of TOTALCHANGE and a variable for the remaining cents. Suitable choices for these could be NUMDOLLARS and NUMCENTS. With these choices made, our variable declaration section will appear as follows:

```
var
    PENNIES,      NICKELS,       DIMES,
    QUARTERS,     HALFDOLLARS,   DOLLARS,
    NUMCENTS,     NUMDOLLARS,    TOTALCHANGE : integer
```

Next consider the process of obtaining the numbers of coins from the user. Specifically, consider the problem of obtaining the number of pennies in the user's pocket. This number will eventually be stored in the variable PENNIES. But how do we get the actual number into that variable? We can't use an assignment statement, since we don't know just how many pennies a user might have. What we use is the READ command. In the case of PENNIES, it would take the form:

```
READ(PENNIES)
```

When this statement is encountered, the Pascal system attempts to obtain an integer *from the keyboard*! Of course, it can only get an integer from the keyboard if the user types one. To tell the user that he or she is expected to type in an integer, we could use a WRITE statement first, thus:

```
WRITE('Number of pennies =');
READ(PENNIES)
```

After the user types the integer representing the number of pennies, the Pascal system stores this integer in the variable PENNIES.

Several variables may be listed in the READ statement. The Pascal system then expects values for each one to be typed in order, with the values separated by spaces or carriage returns. We may use this in the program CHANGE as follows. The program should tell the user (briefly) what it wants, and then READ in the values of the corresponding coins. Assuming the user knows what the program is doing, and in particular knows that the numbers of coins should be typed in the order that we have listed them above, this could be accomplished by the following pair of statements:

```
WRITE('Numbers of coins = ');
READ( PENNIES,      NICKELS,
      DIMES,        QUARTERS,
      HALFDOLLARS,  DOLLARS)
```

At this stage our program would take the form given in Figure 2-3.

```
program CHANGE(INPUT,OUTPUT);
(* --------------------------------------------------------------- *
 *       This program reads in six integer values, respectively    *
 * representing the number of pennies, nickels, dimes, quarters,   *
 * half-dollars, and silver dollars (Susan Bs) in coinage.         *
 *       The program outputs the total value of the coinage        *
 * in dollars and cents.                                           *
 * --------------------------------------------------------------- *)
    var
      PENNIES,        NICKELS,        DIMES,
      QUARTERS,       HALFDOLLARS,    DOLLARS,
      NUMCENTS,       NUMDOLLARS,     TOTALCHANGE : integer;
begin
    WRITE('Numbers of coins = ');
    READ(PENNIES,     NICKELS,
         DIMES,       QUARTERS,
         HALFDOLLARS, DOLLARS);
```

Compute the total value in cents of the coinage;

Compute the total dollars in this value;

Compute the total remaining cents in the value;

Output the results;

```
end.
```

Figure 2-3. CHANGE with Variables and Input Added.

To compute the cents value of the coinage, we must add the number of pennies together with 5 times the number of nickels, together with 10 times the number of dimes, and so on. This value is to be stored in the variable TOTALCHANGE. The following statement achieves this:

```
TOTALCHANGE    :=  PENNIES          + (5 * NICKELS)
               + (10 * DIMES)       + (25 * QUARTERS)
               + (50 * HALFDOLLARS) + (100 * DOLLARS)
```

Now the number of dollars in TOTALCHANGE is just the integer quotient of TOTALCHANGE divided by 100. This is computed by:

```
NUMDOLLARS := TOTALCHANGE div 100
```

And the number of cents in TOTALCHANGE after the dollars are extracted is just the integer remainder on division of TOTALCHANGE by 100. This is computed by:

```
NUMCENTS := TOTALCHANGE mod 100
```

Note that we could also have computed NUMCENTS by:

```
NUMCENTS := TOTALCHANGE - (100 * NUMDOLLARS)
```

At this point our program appears as given in Figure 2-4.

```
program CHANGE(INPUT,OUTPUT);
(* ------------------------------------------------------------ *
 *        This program reads in six integer values, respectively *
 *   representing the number of pennies, nickels, dimes, quarters, *
 *   half-dollars, and silver dollars (Susan Bs) in coinage.      *
 *        The program outputs the total value of the coinage      *
 *   in dollars and cents.                                        *
 * ------------------------------------------------------------ *)
    var
       PENNIES,           NICKELS,          DIMES,
       QUARTERS,          HALFDOLLARS,      DOLLARS,
       NUMCENTS,          NUMDOLLARS,       TOTALCHANGE : integer;
begin
    WRITE('Numbers of coins = ');
    READ(PENNIES,       NICKELS,
         DIMES,         QUARTERS,
         HALFDOLLARS,   DOLLARS);

    TOTALCHANGE    := PENNIES            + (5 * NICKELS)
                    + (10 * DIMES)       + (25 * QUARTERS)
                    + (50 * HALFDOLLARS) + (100 * DOLLARS);

    NUMDOLLARS := TOTALCHANGE div 100;
    NUMCENTS   := TOTALCHANGE mod 100;

    Output the results;

end.
```

Figure 2-4. CHANGE with the Main Computation Refined.

Finally, we will use a WRITE statement to output our results. These must be identified; we use a string for that purpose. We must also print out NUMDOLLARS and NUMCENTS. Since the value of NUMCENTS will be between 0 and 99 (inclusive), we can use the expression

```
NUMCENTS:2
```

to cause it to be printed using only two columns. Similarly, since few people would carry as much as $100 in coinage, we may do the same with NUMDOLLARS. Thus a WRITE statement that will give us a reasonably nice appearing result is

```
WRITE('Change is $', NUMDOLLARS:2, '.', NUMCENTS:2)
```

Our final CHANGE program now appears in Figure 2-5.

```
program CHANGE(INPUT,OUTPUT);
(*  ------------------------------------------------------------  *
 *         This program reads in six integer values, respectively  *
 *   representing the number of pennies, nickels, dimes, quarters,  *
 *   half-dollars, and silver dollars (Susan Bs) in coinage.        *
 *         The program outputs the total value of the coinage       *
 *   in dollars and cents.                                          *
 *  ------------------------------------------------------------  *)
    var
      PENNIES,           NICKELS,          DIMES,
      QUARTERS,          HALFDOLLARS,      DOLLARS,
      NUMCENTS,          NUMDOLLARS,       TOTALCHANGE : integer;
begin
   WRITE('Numbers of coins = ');
   READ(PENNIES,      NICKELS,
        DIMES,        QUARTERS,
        HALFDOLLARS,  DOLLARS);

   TOTALCHANGE    := PENNIES           + (5 * NICKELS)
                   + (10 * DIMES)      + (25 * QUARTERS)
                   + (50 * HALFDOLLARS) + (100 * DOLLARS);

   NUMDOLLARS := TOTALCHANGE div 100;
   NUMCENTS   := TOTALCHANGE mod 100;

   WRITE ('CHANGE IS $', NUMDOLLARS:2, '.', NUMCENTS:2);
end.
```

Figure 2-5. The Complete Program CHANGE.

Below is a sample terminal session from running this program:

```
Numbers of coins = 4 2 3 3 1 1
Change is $ 2.54
```

2.4   Comments and Documentation

As is quite obvious, each of the programs presented in the preceding sections was supplied with a comment describing the program's action. This reflects an important programming principle: all work should be carefully documented. Moreover, this documentation should be prepared as early as possible in the program development process. In particular, the basic description of the program (such as that given in Programs 1-1 and 2-5) should be prepared *before* one single line of Pascal code is produced, even before the development of schematic forms such as Figure 2-2. The reasons for this have grown out of the collective programming experience of the past 35 years.

First of all, it is essential to get the specification of *what* the program is to do precise, correct, and complete before thinking about *how* the program is to achieve any of the desired goals. Human beings that we are, it is often tempting to begin coding portions of the program long before we have completed the (often difficult and painful) process of completely specifying the goals of the program.

Even with programs of relatively small size, this often leads to excessive complication and opaque programs, if not to outright disaster. For it usually occurs that the requirements of other program goals conflict with decisions made in the portions already coded. Then either compromises in the program goals are made (usually not good), or the early code is "patched," and then later "repatched," and so forth. As the program grows in this willy-nilly way, it is soon difficult to see any coherent structure to it, or to understand what it is trying to achieve, or how it is trying to go about it. Often by brute force "change, patch, and modify," programmers can get the program to work for most of the commonly expected inputs. But if the program attempts to do anything beyond the trivial, the programmer is no longer in the position of being able to certify that the program correctly handles *all* inputs. In fact, he or she usually cannot correctly say what it does in general at all! This is a sorry state of affairs whenever the program is expected to do any useful work (which just might be to play games, but to play them correctly!)

So, painful as it may be, it is essential to get the specifications of the program correct at the very outset. If the problem and program are not too complex, these specifications can be included in the program text as an initial comment as we have done so far. When the problem (and program) become substantially more complex, the full description should take the form of a small essay, analyzing the problem. This essay ought to always accompany the program but should not be part of the program text itself.

If your programs are produced solely for your own use, this essay is a useful reminder of what the program is about. It is amazing how fast memory fades as months pass! And if others will use your programs, it is an absolutely essential piece of documentation. Imagine trying to use a complex tool with no manual describing its purposes or operation! If you are extraordinarily clever and persistent (or perverse), you just might be able to work it out. Most likely, you will destroy the tool or something nearby, or simply abandon it in disgust!

These prescriptions may feel slightly silly as you begin working through the first simple programming problems in this text. But work out the specifications anyway! Later problems are sufficiently complex as to require this analysis. But more important, it is essential to cultivate good habits early. The style you develop as you begin to program in a language is most likely the one you will maintain forever. So begin with the right approach, cultivate it, and use it in all your programming work!

Exercises

Exercise 2-1 Calculate each of the following:

    a) 23 * 5 - 2 = ?
    b) 14 - (9 mod 5) = ?
    c) (78 div 19) + (78 mod 19) = ?

Exercise 2-2 Write a small program to calculate the following three quantities:

    345 * (45 + (1978 mod 91))
    (1845 div 34) mod 7
    (-188 * 19) * 456

The output of each calculation should appear on a separate line and should be labeled.

Exercise 2-3 Experiment with the use of the WRITE and WRITELN statements. Write and execute small programs to compare the effects of the following:

    a) WRITE(23, 45)
       with
       WRITE(23); WRITE(45).
    b) WRITE('Slithy toves gyre', 'quickly')
       with
       WRITE('Slithy toves gyre', 'quickly').
    c) WRITE('Slithy toves gyre', 'quickly')
       with
       WRITE('Slithy toves gyre'); WRITE('quickly').

Exercise 2-4 Write a simple tax program called TAKEHOME. The input to the program is to be the user's annual salary. The output is to be the user's weekly salary, after taxes have been withheld. Use a tax withholding rate of 20% (or any other irrational figure).

Chapter Three

But There's Much More to Talk about: Real Numbers, Characters, and Other Things

"The time has come," the Walrus said,
  "To talk of many things:
Of shoes – and ships – and sealing-wax –
  Of cabbages – and kings – "

Lewis Carroll
Through the Looking Glass

There are indeed a great many things to talk about with your computer besides integers. In this chapter we will consider some of them. The topics will include:

- Representing real numbers in Pascal.
- Operations on real numbers.

- Using variables for real numbers.
- Characters and their codes.
- Boolean values and Boolean operations.
- Declaring and using enumeration types.

3.1   Taking the World's Measure

In the last chapter we introduced integers and used them to talk about money. Such talk is typical of the use of integers: the subject of conversation is discrete and can be counted precisely. However, much of what is interesting and important to talk about is continuous and can only be measured approximately, such as the lengths of lines, the sizes of angles, the voltages of currents, the speeds of vehicles, the thicknesses of films, and so on.

The fundamental tool for using and measuring such quantities is the notion of a *real number*. Thus we hear such phrases as:

a line of 213.41 inches
an angle of 34.9 degrees
a current of –5.15 volts
a speed of 67.2 mph
a film of thickness 0.004 cm

Fortunately, Pascal allows us the same form of expression for real numbers as we find in everyday life. Thus

213.41,   34.9,   –5.15,   67.2,   and   0.004

are all acceptable descriptions of real numbers in Pascal.

There is another acceptable form for real numbers: the so-called *scientific* or *floating point* notation. In this style, real numbers are expressed in the form

nnEmm

where *nn* and *mm* are integers with or without plus or minus signs. This notation is understood as an abbreviation of the number:

$$nn * 10^{mm}$$

Consequently, the examples given above can be rendered as:

2.1341E2,   3.49E1,   –5.15E0,   6.72E1,   and   4.0E-3

Real numbers can be operated upon with the standard arithmetic operations of addition, subtraction, multiplication, and division. Thus such expressions as

34.9 + 3.07,   (-5.15)*2.0,   and   67.2/3.1

are all acceptable Pascal expressions and have their usual meanings.

Integers and real numbers may be mixed together in the arithmetic operations +, -, *, and /. In the case of /, the result is always a real number. In the cases of +, -, and *, if both arguments are integers, the result is an integer. Otherwise, the result is a real number.

In addition to these arithmetic operations, standard Pascal provides six mathematical operations or functions. These are:

ln(x)	=	the natural logarithm of x
		(the logarithm of x in base e);
exp(x)	=	the exponential of x
	=	(e to the power x);
sqrt(x)	=	the square root of x;
sin(x)	=	the trigonometric sine of x;
cos(x)	=	the trigonometric cosine of x;
arctan(x)	=	the angle whose tangent is x.

In the last three functions, the angles are measured in radians. You will recall that the degree measure and radian measure of the same angle are related by the proportion:

radians/2*PI = degrees/360.

Variables for real numbers are similar to variables for integers. They are conceptual containers capable of containing real numbers. To declare that an identifier is to be used for a real variable, we use a declaration of the form:

identifier: real

As before, several identifiers may be included in the same declaration by placing them together before the colon, separating the individual identifiers by commas. Thus

OPPOSITE, ADJACENT, ANGLE : real;

is an acceptable declaration of three real variables.

Now consider the following problem. We need a program that will read in the lengths of the legs of a right triangle and print out the size of one of the angles between the hypotenuse and one of the legs. First recall the definition of tangent. Let ANGLE be the size of the angle in question and let OPP and ADJ be the lengths of the sides opposite to and adjacent to the given angle:

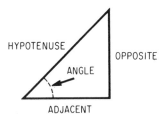

Then

      tangent (ANGLE) = OPP/ADJ

so that

      ANGLE = arctan (OPP/ADJ).

For our program we will need three real variables. Two of them, OPPOSITE and ADJACENT, will be used for the lengths of the legs, while the third, ANGLE, will be used for the size of one of the angles of interest. Thus the preceding declaration will be suitable for this program. We can now outline the program as given in Figure 3-1.

```
program ANGLE(INPUT,OUTPUT);
(*  ------------------------------------------------------------  *
 *        This program inputs the lengths of the two legs of a    *
 *   right triangle and calculates the angle between one of the   *
 *   sides and the hypotenuse of the triangle. The first input    *
 *   is the length of the side opposite the angle to be calculated, *
 *   and the second input is the length of the side adjacent to the *
 *   angle to be calculated.                                      *
 *        The output of the program is the size of the angle      *
 *   expressed in both radians and degrees.                       *
 *  ------------------------------------------------------------  *)
    var
        OPPOSITE, ADJACENT, ANGLE : real;

begin

    Input the lengths of the two legs;

    Calculate the measure of one angle;

    Output the result;

end.
```

Figure 3-1.   Outline of the Program ANGLE.

Now we must refine the non-Pascal portions of this outline. The READ and WRITE statements are capable of dealing with real numbers just as well as with integers and literals. Thus the process of input and output for reals is just like that for integers. There is only one small difference. This difference is in the control of the output. If a WRITE statement is used to output a real number, and if no control information is attached concerning the format of that number, it is assumed that the floating point or scientific form is desired. To obtain the common form of real numbers, one proceeds as follows: if the real expression to be written out is *re*, and if one uses

WRITE(re:n:m)

then the real number will be written in the usual form, using n columns overall, and using m columns for the decimal part (that is, the part to the right of the decimal point). Thus to print *re* with six columns overall and two for the decimal part, one would use:

WRITE(*re* : 6 : 2)

Using these observations, we will be able to easily refine the input and output portions of the outline program. There remains the problem of calculating the angle. As we observed above, the basic relation is:

ANGLE = arctan(OPP/ADJ).

Since the program will have input these lengths using the variables OPPOSITE and ADJACENT, it is easy to calculate the quantity OPPOSITE/ADJACENT. But now we can make use of the mathematical function arctan, which is supplied by standard Pascal. When supplied with a real number, arctan returns the measure (in radians) of an angle with that tangent. Consequently, we may refine the program as indicated in Program 3-1.

```
program ANGLE(INPUT,OUTPUT);
(*  ----------------------------------------------------------------- *
 *        This program inputs the lengths of the two legs of a        *
 *   right triangle and calculates the angle between one of the       *
 *   sides and the hypotenuse of the triangle. The first input        *
 *   is the length of the side opposite the angle to be calculated,   *
 *   and the second input is the length of the side adjacent to the   *
 *   angle to be calculated.                                          *
 *        The output of the program is the size of the angle          *
 *   expressed in both radians and degrees.                           *
 *  ----------------------------------------------------------------- *)
    var
        OPPOSITE, ADJACENT, ANGLE : real;

begin

    WRITE('Opposite side =');
    READ(OPPOSITE);

    WRITE('Adjacent side =');
    READ(ADJACENT);

    ANGLE := ARCTAN(OPPOSITE/ADJACENT);

    WRITELN('Angle = ', ANGLE:5:2, ' radians');

end.
```

Program 3-1. A Program for Computing Angles.

If we wish to obtain the results in both radians and degrees, we need only recall the relation:

radians/2*PI = degrees/360.

From this it follows that

degrees = (radians * 180)/PI,

and so we may produce the final program as follows (Program 3-2):

```
program ANGLE(INPUT,OUTPUT);
(* ------------------------------------------------------------- *
 *        This program inputs the lengths of the two legs of a   *
 * right triangle and calculates the angle between one of the    *
 * sides and the hypotenuse of the triangle. The first input     *
 * is the length of the side opposite the angle to be calculated,*
 * and the second input is the length of the side adjacent to the*
 * angle to be calculated.                                       *
 *        The output of the program is the size of the angle     *
 * expressed in both radians and degrees.                        *
 * ------------------------------------------------------------- *)
    const
       PI = 3.1416;
    var
       OPPOSITE, ADJACENT, ANGLE : real;

begin

    WRITE('Opposite side =');
    READ(OPPOSITE);
    WRITE('Adjacent side =');
    READ(ADJACENT);
    ANGLE := ARCTAN(OPPOSITE/ADJACENT);
    WRITELN('Angle = ', ANGLE:5:2, ' radians');
    WRITELN('Angle = ', (180 * ANGLE)/PI:5:2, ' degrees');

end.
```

Program 3-2. A Program for Computing Angles.

We have included one more new usage in Program 3-2. This is a *constant declaration*, which occurs before the variable declaration. As its name suggests, a constant declaration establishes an identifier as a name for a fixed individual value. Such constant declarations must occur in the constant declaration section which is introduced by the reserved word *const*. This section must be the first of the declaration sections when it occurs in a program. (As the example of Program 1-1 shows, the constant declaration section is not required in Pascal programs.) The individual constant declarations have the form:

identifier = constant;

Signed or unsigned numbers (both integer and real) are constants. Thus the following are acceptable constant declarations:

```
VELOCITYLIGHT        =  2.99793E10;
MICRON               =  1E-4;
TWOEXP20             =  1048576;
MELTPOINTNEON        =  -249;
```

The use of constant declarations improves the readability of programs by clearly indicating the meaning of particular numerical values that occur in the program. Their use also improves the usefulness of programs by making them more adaptable to changing circumstances. Often constants are subject to revision. Even more often, programs will employ constants that are relatively arbitrary, depending on the intended application of a program. For example, in printing bills for a company, constants might be used to describe the size of various sections of the bill, thus controlling the printing process. When the company shifts to a different size bill, the program can be easily adapted simply by changing the constant declarations, rather than wading through the entire program to find and change the occurrences of the numerical values.

3.2   Messages and Codes

As we have seen, literals or strings (that is, sequences of characters enclosed in single quotes) can be used in conjunction with the WRITE statement to output messages from programs. However, Pascal does not provide any standard literal or string variables for inputting such literals. Yet there are many applications in which one would like to deal with text and characters.   First, there are many circumstances in which one desires responses such as YES or NO from the user of a program in order to respond correctly. Other programs must directly manipulate text and characters. Automatic text and letter formatting programs ("wordprocessors") as well as program translators must do this.

Though Pascal does not provide a "literal variable" capability, it does provide the facility to deal with characters. Specifically, Pascal provides a standard type of entity which amounts to the printing character set used to communicate with the computer. The name for this type is the reserved word *char*. Unfortunately, the exact contents of this type varies considerably from computer to computer for the simple reason that the character sets of different computers vary. But at minimum, the type char is supposed to include the upper case Roman letters (A,B, . . . ,Z), the digits (0,1, . . . ,9), the blank space, and various special characters such as %, #, and so forth. On many computers it also includes the lower case letters as well as a wide range of special characters.

Individual characters enclosed in single quotes are constants. Thus 'A' and '9' are constants. Therefore, the following would be acceptable constant declarations:

```
· FIRSTLETTER = 'A';
  NINE        = '9';
```

As with the types integer and real (and in fact with any type Pascal recognizes), one can declare variables that range over the type. For type char, these declarations take the form:

identifier : char;

Thus

```
NEXTCHAR : char;
```

is an acceptable declaration of a char variable. Having declared a char variable, we may assign to it and obtain values from it. Thus both

```
NEXTCHAR := 'A'
```

and

```
NEXTCHAR := FIRSTLETTER
```

would assign the letter A to the variable NEXTCHAR, provided of course that the constant declaration indicated above had been made. On the other hand, the statement

```
WRITE(NEXTCHAR)
```

would cause the letter A to be printed on the terminal or in the output file.

As a small, simple example, consider a program that is to read five characters from the INPUT file and write the same five characters in reverse order on the OUTPUT file. Program 3-3, which uses five distinct char variables, does just this.

```
program TAKEFIVE(INPUT,OUTPUT);
(*  ------------------------------------------------------------  *
 *        This program reads in five characters and prints them  *
 *  back out in reverse order.                                   *
 *  ------------------------------------------------------------  *)
     var
        CHAR1,CHAR2,CHAR3,CHAR4,CHAR5 : char;

begin
    WRITE('Input characters = ');
    READ(CHAR1, CHAR2, CHAR3, CHAR4, CHAR5);
    WRITELN('Result = ', CHAR5, CHAR4, CHAR3, CHAR2, CHAR1);

end.
```

Program 3-3.   A Program to Read and Reverse Five Characters.

The character set or type char is always listed in some definite order, which unfortunately is as variable as that of the character sets themselves. All that can be assumed is that the letters are in alphabetical order and that the digits are in their natural order. But whether the digits occur before or after the letters, and where the blank and other special characters occur, is very much dependent on the particular computer.   Whatever the particulars of this order, Pascal provides us with a means for utilizing it. In fact, it really provides two methods.   The first is simply that one can use the ordering symbols

> $<$, $>$, $<=$, $>=$, $=$ and $<>$

between expressions designating characters. Thus one can write

```
'A' < 'C'
NEXTCHAR >= '8'
FIRSTLETTER <= '%'
```

These expressions may be either true or false. That is, they are *Boolean-valued* operators. (We will study Boolean values in detail in the next section.)

The second method simply notes that there must be a first character in the list, a second, and so forth. With this observation, Pascal provides a standard function ORD(. . .), which maps characters into integers, taking the first character of the list onto 1, the second onto 2, and so on.

Thus if 'A' is the first character of the list, then ORD('A') = 1, while ORD('Y') = 25. Pascal also provides the inverse function CHR(. . .). For integers in the appropriate range, ORD(n) yields the character c such that ORD(c) = n. Thus under the assumption above, CHR(1) = 'A' and CHR(25) = 'Y'.

Finally, Pascal also provides a predecessor and a successor function for characters in the list. These are the functions PRED(. . .) and SUCC(. . .), respectively. Thus, if c is *not* the first character in the list, then PRED(c) is the character immediately preceding c. If c is not the *last* character in the list, then SUCC(c) is the character immediately following c. Consequently, PRED('C') = 'B' and SUCC('E') = 'F'. By its definition PRED(. . .) is undefined for the first character in the list, and SUCC(. . .) is undefined for the last character in the list.

From the definitions given, it is easy to see that (for the appropriate n), the following hold whenever they make sense at all:

```
CHR(ORD(C)) = C
ORD(CHR(N)) = N
PRED(C)  = CHR(ORD(C)-1)
SUCC(C)  = CHR(ORD(C)+1)
```

We will make serious use of char variables in Chapter 6, where we will write a note-taking program, and in Chapter 10, where we will write a program to format the comments in Pascal programs into neat little boxes.

3.3   Other Things

The remaining standard type we have not yet met consists of only two objects: the *truth-values* true and false. The type is named *Boolean* (in honor of George Boole). The significance of these objects lies in their use in decision-making, which we will take up in detail in Chapters 4 and 5. For the moment it suffices to note that we may declare variables ranging over this type and that Pascal provides a number of operators mapping truth-values into truth-values. To declare that an identifier is to be associated with a Boolean variable, we use the now familiar format as follows:

identifier : Boolean;

As with all the other types, we may deal with several identifiers at once, separating them with commas. Thus

    TEST, FLAG : Boolean;

is an example of a declaration of two Boolean variables. Given these declarations, the following are acceptable assignment statements:

    TEST := true;
    FLAG := false;
    TEST := FLAG;

Boolean values, Boolean variables, and Boolean expressions (defined below) may all be used in WRITE statements. Thus

    WRITE(true,FLAG)

would cause

    true false

to be printed, provided that FLAG had been assigned the value false. Unfortunately, Boolean variables may not occur in READ statements in standard Pascal.

Pascal's built-in Boolean operators are: and, or, not. Their actions are described by the following tables:

and	true false	*or*	true false	*not*	
true	true false	true	true true	true	false
false	false false	false	true false	false	true

Utilizing these tables and the declarations above, consider the following sequence of assignments:

    TEST := true;
    FLAG := (TEST and false);
    TEST := (FLAG or not(TEST))

Of course, after the first assignment, TEST contains the value true. After the second, FLAG contains the value false. And after the third, TEST contains the value false.

As the last assignment indicates, the Boolean operators may be nested together, as long as one uses parentheses to group the operations (just as with arithmetic operators). Thus one may write

    TEST := not(TEST or FLAG)

as well as

```
TEST := (not(TEST) and not(FLAG))
```

In this case, the two assignments have the same effect.

Earlier, we introduced the relational operators <, >, <=, >=, =, <> for use with numbers and characters. Any particular statement (such as 33 < 14) was interpreted as being either true or false in the usual intuitive sense. In fact, however, the operators really do produce output, namely one of the Boolean values true or false. Thus they can be used in assignment statements. Given the declarations made above,

```
TEST := 33 < 14;
FLAG := (4.3 >= 3.4)
```

will have the effect of assigning the value false to TEST and the value true to FLAG.

Up to this point, we have encountered four types of entities in Pascal: the types integer, real, char, and Boolean. These are all simple types in the sense that the entities in them (e.g., integers) are simple and thus have no internal structure. Such simple entities are called *scalars*, and hence types whose elements are scalars are called *scalar types*. Thus types integer, real, char, and Boolean are all scalar types. In later chapters we will learn how to define non-scalar or *structured* types.

The types integer, real, char, and Boolean are also *standard* in the sense that they are automatically provided by Pascal. However, it is often useful to be able to use scalar types other than the standard ones. For this reason, Pascal enables programmers to define new scalar types by means of *type declarations*. (We will later define structured types by such declarations.) Such programmer-defined scalar types are called *enumeration types*, since they are defined by listing or enumerating the scalars that are to belong in the type. Just as numbers, characters, and Booleans have names by which we refer to them, so too must the scalars of an enumeration type. These names are whatever the programmer chooses when the type is defined or declared.

For example, suppose we were designing a program which for one reason or another had to deal with the days of the week for a considerable amount of time. (Perhaps it is a pupil attendance program in a school or a scheduling program in a public building or university.) In Pascal, we may define a type WEEK as follows:

```
type
   WEEK = (SUN, MON, TUES, WED, THURS, FRI, SAT);
```

Thus in this Pascal program, the identifiers "SUN," "MON," and so forth will be used as names for the days of the week. Of course, the actual days of the week (whatever they really are) are no more "inside" the computer than the actual integers (whatever they really are). In both cases, the computer manipulates electronic representatives of the real entities.

As this example indicates, type declarations must be introduced by the reserved word *type*. All the type declarations of a program (if any) must be collected together (separating them with semicolons) and must occur after the constant declarations (if any) and before the variable declarations.

We may declare variables to range over enumeration types, just as with any other type. Thus, given the type declaration of WEEK above,

```
var
    TODAY,TOMORROW : WEEK;
```

declares that TODAY and TOMORROW are variables ranging over the type WEEK. Then such assignment statements as

```
TODAY := WED;
TOMORROW := TODAY
```

are acceptable Pascal statements.

While we will see that enumeration types can be quite helpful, their utility is considerably reduced by the fact that standard Pascal does not permit their elements in WRITE statements, nor does it permit variables over them in READ statements. Thus they may not be used directly in input and output operations. Extensions of Pascal which permit their use in input and output operations are very desirable.

In the case of the standard scalar types, the rules for manipulating them are built into the system. In the case of the programmer-defined scalar types, the rules are largely what the programmer specifies in the program. However, Pascal does provide a few bits of basic machinery for manipulating enumeration types. This machinery is similar to some of that used for the type char.

Since an enumeration type is given by listing its members in a definite order (the one actually used in the program), Pascal provides a function ord(. . .) that will output the corresponding integer for each member of the type. Thus for the type week declared above, we would have ord(SUN) = 1 and ord(WED) = 4.

Pascal also allows the use of the ordering relation symbols ($<$, $>$, $<=$, $>=$, $=$, $<>$) with enumeration types. The truth or falsity of any particular statement is determined by the ordering in which the type was defined. Thus (SUN $<$ TUES) is a true statement, while (WED $<$ MON) is a false statement. As we noted in our discussion of Boolean values, the ordering symbols really denote Boolean operators that can be used in assignment statements. Thus if TEST and FLAG have been declared to be Boolean variables, the assignments

```
if (SUN < TUES) then TEST := true else TEST := false;
if (WED < MON)  then FLAG := true else FLAG := false
```

will have the effect of assigning true to the variable TEST and false to the variable FLAG.

Finally, Pascal provides two other operators on enumeration types to allow one to find the predecessor and successor of a scalar (when they exist). These are the functions pred(. . .) and succ(. . .). The first is defined for all elements of an enumeration type except the very first element. In all cases where it is defined, pred(. . .) yields the immediate predecessor of its input. Thus pred(TUES) = MON. The other function is defined for all elements of an enumeration type except for the very last. And as you would expect, succ(. . .) gives out the immediate successor of its input when it is defined. Hence succ(TUES) = WED.

Exercises

Exercise 3-1   Determine whether the results of each of the following is an integer or real number:

  a) 34 * 19
  b) 4 + 3.7
  c) 10/5
  d) 7.0 - 4

Exercise 3-2   Write the scientific or floating-point representation of each of the following real numbers:

  a) -1423.97
  b) 0.00098

Exercise 3-3   Write the usual representation of the following real numbers:

  a) -15.729E-4
  b) 9.73E5

Exercise 3-4   Write a program LEGS that accepts as input the length of the hypotenuse of a right triangle together with the size in radians of one of the (non-right) angles. The output of the program is to be the lengths of the two legs of the triangle. Recall that in terms of the figure on page 37,

  OPP = HYP * sin(ANGLE)   and   ADJ = HYP * cos(ANGLE)

Exercise 3-5 Modify the program LEGS of Exercise 3-4 so that the size of the angle input is expressed in degrees.

Exercise 3-6   A ball thrown upward from the surface of the earth with an initial velocity of V0 feet per second will be at height

  p(t) = (-0.5 * G * t * t) + (V0 * t)

feet above the earth t seconds after it is released. Here G is the gravitational constant G = 32.2 feet/sec/sec. Its velocity t seconds after release will be

$$v(t) \quad + \quad -G * t + V0.$$

Write a program that will accept as input the initial velocity together with a time in seconds. The output of the program is to be the position and velocity of the ball at that time.

Chapter Four

Repetitive Conversations: Iteration

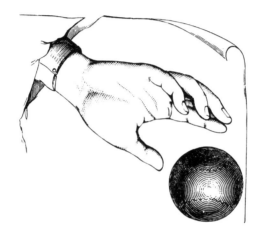

Thus far we have mainly discussed *topics* for conversation in Pascal. Now we will consider how to take more *control* of the conversation. Our first method will be to learn to repeat various acts. In ordinary conversation, repetition is not very desirable. But in Pascal, not only is such repetition acceptable; it constitutes one of the most powerful tools at the programmer's disposal. The topics considered in this chapter include the following:

- Repeating an action a fixed number of times.
- Iterating actions an indefinite number of times.
- Using Boolean conditions to control iteration.

4.1 Limited Repetition

As we pointed out earlier, computers have a very limited repertoire of primitive acts they can carry out. Their great power comes from being able to carry out these simple acts very quickly. To be able to harness this speed, we must be able to instruct the machine to repeatedly carry out the same act for a variety of different inputs, for example, to tell it to compute the monthly bills for each customer in a certain list or to calculate the grade average for each pupil in a given class, and so forth. Pascal provides several methods for accomplishing this task. The first of these is the *for statement*. Suppose we wish to multiply the numbers from 1 to 12 together. If we have previously declared NUM and PROD to be integer variables, we can achieve our goal with the following two statements:

```
PROD  :=  1;
for NUM  :=  1 to 12 do
    PROD  :=  PROD * NUM
```

We are already well acquainted with assignment statements, so the first of these gives us no trouble. The second really does just what it says. It first sets NUM to 1 and executes the following assignment statement. Then it increments NUM to 2 and again executes the assignment statement, and so forth. It executes the assignment statement for each of the values NUM = 1,2,3, . . . ,12, in order. Thus the values of PROD are successively 1,2,6,24,120, . . . up to PROD = 479,001,600.

The general form of the *for* statement is

```
for ident  := start to stop do
    statement
```

Now we must explain the various parts of this compound. The values *start* and *stop* must be scalars from the same type. In our example, they are integers. But they could both be characters, or Booleans, or they could belong to an enumeration type. However, they cannot be real numbers. The expression *ident* must be a variable that has been declared to range over the same type from which *start* and *stop* have been drawn. Finally, *statement* must be an acceptable Pascal statement. Up to this point we have encountered assignment statements together with the READ and WRITE statements. But now we have added the for statement to that list, and later we will add others. *Any* of these is acceptable as the *statement* in the for statement given above.

If we have at hand the type declaration of WEEK given in our discussion of enumeration types in Chapter 3, and if we have declared DAY to be a variable of type WEEK, then the following would be acceptable in Pascal:

```
for DAY := SUN to SAT do
    WRITE(ord(DAY))
```

The effect of this statement would be to print out the numbers 1 through 7. It acts as follows. The variable DAY is first set to SUN, and the WRITE statement is executed. Then the variable DAY is incremented to MON using the succ(. . .) function on the type WEEK, and the WRITE statement is again executed. Then DAY is incremented to TUES by once more using succ(. . .), and so forth. This continues until DAY has been set to SAT and the WRITE statement given its last execution.

To incorporate these considerations into a complete program, let us consider the problem of computing the odds of obtaining k heads in n tosses of a fair coin. Let us call this probability p(k,n). Then the theory of probability tells us that $p(0,n) = (\frac{1}{2})^{**}n$, where $2^{**}n$ is 2 raised to the power n, and if we have already been able to calculate p(k,n), then we can obtain p(k+1,n) from the equality

```
p(k+1,n) = [ (n-k) / (k+1) ] * p(k,n)
```

This suggests the approach to designing our program as given in Figure 4-1.

```
program COINODDS(INPUT,OUTPUT);
(* ------------------------------------------------------------ *
 *         This program calculates the odds p(k,n) of getting   *
 * exactly k heads in n tosses of a fair coin. It uses the      *
 * relations:                                                   *
 *                                                              *
 *         p(0,n) = (½)**n                                       *
 * and                                                          *
 *         p(k+1,n) = [ (n-k) / (k+1) ] * p(k,n),                *
 *                                                              *
 * where 2**n is 2 raised to the power n.                       *
 *         The input to the program is a pair of integers indicating *
 * the number of tosses and the number of heads.                *
 *         The output from the program is the odds of obtaining *
 * exactly that number of heads in that many tosses.            *
 * ------------------------------------------------------------ *)
begin

    Obtain the numbers of tosses and heads;

    First calculate p(0,NUMTOSS);

    Now calculate p(NUMHEAD,NUMTOSS);

    Output the results;
end.
```

Figure 4-1.   Outline of a Program to Compute Coin Odds.

Now our problem is to refine the non-Pascal statements in this outline into acceptable Pascal code. The first decision to make is the choice of necessary variables. Obviously we need integer variables for the numbers of tosses and numbers of heads. The identifiers NUMTOSS and NUMHEAD would be suitable for these. We will also need a real variable to hold the probability, which is the goal of the computation. The identifier PROBABILITY is a suitable choice for this. By now we are familiar with the processes of input and output. Thus we can consider our first refinement, as presented in Figure 4-2.

```
program COINODDS(INPUT,OUTPUT);
(* ------------------------------------------------------------ *
 *        This program calculates the odds p(k,n) of getting    *
 * exactly k heads in n tosses of a fair coin. It uses the      *
 * relations:                                                   *
 *                                                              *
 *        p(0,n) = (½)**n                                        *
 * and                                                          *
 *        p(k+1,n) = [ (n-k) / (k+1) ] * p(k,n),                *
 * where 2**n is 2 raised to the power n.                       *
 *        The input to the program is a pair of integers indicating *
 * the number of tosses and the number of heads.               *
 *        The output from the program is the odds of obtaining  *
 * exactly that number of heads in that many tosses.           *
 * ------------------------------------------------------------ *)
    var
       PROBABILITY : real;
       NUMTOSS, NUMHEAD, COUNT : integer;

begin

    WRITE ('Number of tosses = ');
    READ (NUMTOSS);
    WRITE ('Number of heads = ');
    READ (NUMHEAD);

    First calculate p(0,NUMTOSS);

    Now calculate p(NUMHEAD,NUMTOSS);

    WRITELN('The probability of obtaining exactly ',
            NUMHEAD:3, ' heads in ');
    WRITELN(NUMTOSS:3, ' coin tosses is ', PROBABILITY:8:6);
end.
```

Figure 4-2. First Refinement of the Program COINODDS

Next let us consider the computation of p(0,NUMTOSS). According to our basic relation, this value is $1/(2^{**}\text{NUMTOSS})$. This is equivalent to $(0.5)^{**}\text{NUMTOSS}$. That is, we must calculate

$$0.5 * 0.5 * 0.5 * \ldots * 0.5$$

where there are NUMTOSS many factors in this product. One way to do this would be to first set PROBABILITY to 1.0 and then to repeatedly multiply this by 0.5 – NUMTOSS many times. Repeatedly executing a simple act is just what the for statement is designed to do. To use it, we need some sort of variable for the loop to act upon – the *ident* of our schematic form. Since the *start* and *stop* of this statement will be 1 and NUMTOSS, which are integers, this variable must also be an integer. Let us use COUNT for this variable. Of course, we will have to declare COUNT to be an integer variable in our program. But presuming this is done, the following code will compute the value of p(0,NUMTOSS), leaving the required value in the variable PROBABILITY:

```
PROBABILITY := 1;
for COUNT := 1 to NUMTOSS do
    PROBABILITY := PROBABILITY * 0.5
```

Now we may apply much the same strategy to compute p(NUMHEAD,NUMTOSS). After the code just presented is executed, the variable PROBABILITY holds the value p(0,NUMTOSS). So now we must use the second part of our basic relation so as to compute

$$p(0,\text{NUMTOSS}), p(1,\text{NUMTOSS}), \ldots, p(\text{NUMHEAD},\text{NUMTOSS})$$

in the order indicated. At each step, according to our basic relation,

$$p(k+1,\text{NUMTOSS}) = ((\text{NUMTOSS}-k)/(k+1)) * p(k,\text{NUMTOSS}).$$

Once more, this is a repetitive computation – the sort easily dealt with in for statements. Note that we must let k range from 0 to NUMTOSS-1. For when k = NUMTOSS-1, then k+1 = NUMTOSS. Since at the outset of this work PROBABILITY holds p(0,NUMTOSS), we can use it to hold each of the successive values of p(k,NUMTOSS). Using COUNT for k, the following code will lnow carry the computation forward:

```
for COUNT := 0 to NUMHEAD-1 do
    PROBABILITY := ((NUMTOSS-COUNT)/(COUNT+1)) * PROBABILITY
```

We can now use these observations to carry out the final refinements of our outline for COINODDS. Our final program is presented in Program 4-1.

```
program COINODDS(INPUT,OUTPUT);
(* ---------------------------------------------------------------- *
 *        This program calculates the odds p(k,n) of getting         *
 *  exactly k heads in n tosses of a fair coin. It uses the          *
 *  relations:                                                       *
 *                                                                   *
 *        p(0,n) = (½)**n                                             *
 *  and                                                              *
 *        p(k+1,n) = [ (n-k) / (k+1) ] * p(k,n),                      *
 *  where 2**n is 2 raised to the power n.                           *
 *        The input to the program is a pair of integers indicating  *
 *  the number of tosses and the number of heads.                    *
 *        The output from the program is the odds of obtaining       *
 *  exactly that number of heads in that many tosses.                *
 * ---------------------------------------------------------------- *)
     var
         PROBABILITY : real;
         NUMTOSS, NUMHEAD, COUNT : integer;

begin

     WRITE ('Number of tosses = ');
     READ (NUMTOSS);
     WRITE ('Number of heads = ');
     READ (NUMHEAD);

     (* First calculate p(0,NUMTOSS) *)

     PROBABILITY := 1.0 ;
     for COUNT := 1 to NUMTOSS do
         PROBABILITY := PROBABILITY * 0.5 ;

     (* Now calculate p(NUMHEAD,NUMTOSS)  *)

     for COUNT := 0 to NUMHEAD-1 do
         PROBABILITY := ((NUMTOSS-COUNT) / (COUNT+1)) * PROBABILITY;

     WRITELN('The probability of obtaining exactly ',
             NUMHEAD:3, ' heads in ');
     WRITELN(NUMTOSS:3,' coin tosses is ', PROBABILITY:8:6);
end.
```

Program 4-1.   The Complete Program COINODDS.

Pascal admits another form of the for statement, specifically:

for *ident* := *start* downto *stop* do
    statement

The only difference between this form and the original is that at each cycle, instead of incrementing *ident*, the system decrements it, either by subtracting 1 if it is an integer or by using the pred(. . .) function in other cases.

4.2 Going on Forever

The sort of iteration that the for statement deals with so well can be described as *definite iteration*, since the number of times the given statement is executed is definitely fixed before the for statement commences execution. There are, however, many situations in which one must repeat an action an unknown number of times. For example, consider the age-old problem: if I start with S dollars and my money doubles every year, how long will it take until I have at least G dollars? What is to be calculated here is how many times the elementary act of doubling the money must be repeated. So to solve a problem of this sort, we need some method of indefinite iteration. Pascal provides this in the while and repeat statements. Consider the following:

```
while CURRENTVALUE < GOALAMOUNT do
    CURRENTVALUE := 2 * CURRENTVALUE
```

Suppose CURRENTVALUE contains the value S (dollars) before this code is reached. Then the effect of executing the preceding fragment above is that as long as the CURRENTVALUE remains below GOALAMOUNT (which presumably contains the value G), CURRENT-VALUE is repeatedly doubled.

The general form of the while statement is

while *condition* do
statement

Here *condition* is any Boolean expression: a Boolean constant (true or false), a Boolean variable, a relational expression, or a compound built up out of these by means of the Boolean operators and, or, not. And *statement* is *any* acceptable Pascal statement. The general effect of executing a while statement is that the *statement* portion is repeatedly executed as long as the *condition* is true. Specifically, the *condition* is first checked, and if it is true, then the *statement* is executed; then the condition is tested again and so forth until the *condition* becomes false. Of course it is presumed that something in the execution of *statement* has the potential to alter the truth-value of *condition*. Otherwise, once begun, the while statement will never stop and will execute infinitely (or at least until you "pull the plug" by some means or other).

These considerations suggest the following outline solution to our problem:

```
program DOUBLING(INPUT,OUTPUT);
(*  ----------------------------------------------------------------- *
 *        This program takes two real number inputs:STARTING-          *
 *  AMOUNT and GOALAMOUNT. It assumes that STARTINGAMOUNT is to        *
 *  be doubled and redoubled, etc., every YEAR.                        *
 *        The output of the program is the number of YEARs of such     *
 *  doubling and redoubling until the original STARTINGAMOUNT has      *
 *  grown at least as large as the GOALAMOUNT.                         *
 *  ----------------------------------------------------------------- *)
    var
        YEAR : INTEGER;
        STARTINGAMOUNT, GOALAMOUNT, CURRENTVALUE : REAL;

begin
    Obtain STARTINGAMOUNT and GOALAMOUNT;

    Initialize CURRENTVALUE and YEAR;

    Repeatedly double CURRENTAMOUNT until its value is at
        least GOALMOUNT, incrementing YEAR each time;

    Output the results;

end.
```

Figure 4-3. Outline of the Program DOUBLING.

The process of refining this outline is straightforward. The input and output portions will present no difficulty nor will the initialization statements since they will just be assignments. To deal with the main computational part, we need only make the following observation. Pascal permits us to bundle any number of individual statements into a *compound* statement. If S1, . . . , Sk are Pascal statements, then

```
begin S1 ; S2 ; . . . ; Sk end
```

is an acceptable Pascal statement and is called a *compound* statement. Notice that the component statements are separated by semicolons surrounded by the "super-parentheses" begin . . . end. The effect of executing a compound statement is simply to execute the component statements in the order indicated.

Now we can finish refining the main computational part of the program DOUBLING. The action we must repeatedly execute has two components: we must double CURRENTVALUE and we must increment YEAR. These two acts can be bundled into the following compound statement:

```
begin
  CURRENTVALUE := 2 * CURRENTVALUE;
  YEAR := YEAR + 1
end
```

Since the *statement* portion of a while statement can be *any* legal Pascal statement we can use this compound statement. Thus the main computational part of our program becomes

```
while CURRENTVALUE < GOALAMOUNT do
  begin
    CURRENTVALUE := 2 * CURRENTVALUE;
    YEAR := YEAR + 1
  end
```

Thus our final version of DOUBLING appears as Program 4-2.

```
program DOUBLING(INPUT,OUTPUT);
(*  ------------------------------------------------------------  *
 *        This program takes two real number inputs: STARTING-    *
 *  AMOUNT and GOALAMOUNT. It assumes that STARTINGAMOUNT is to    *
 *  be doubled and redoubled, etc., every YEAR.                   *
 *        The output of the program is the number of YEARs of such *
 *  doubling and redoubling until the original STARTINGAMOUNT has *
 *  grown at least as large as the GOALAMOUNT.                    *
 *  ------------------------------------------------------------  *)
    var
       YEAR : INTEGER;
       STARTINGAMOUNT, GOALAMOUNT, CURRENTVALUE : REAL;
begin
   WRITE('STARTING AMOUNT =');
   READ(STARTINGAMOUNT);

   WRITE('GOAL AMOUNT =');
   READ(GOALAMOUNT);

   YEAR := 0;
   CURRENTVALUE := STARTINGAMOUNT;

   while CURRENTVALUE < GOALAMOUNT do
      begin
         CURRENTVALUE := CURRENTVALUE * 2;
         YEAR := YEAR + 1;
      end;

   WRITELN('DOUBLING EVERY YEAR, $', STARTINGAMOUNT:8:2,
           ' WILL REACH OR EXCEED $', GOALAMOUNT:8:2,
           ' AFTER ',   YEAR:4,    ' YEARS.'   );

end.
```

Program 4-2. The DOUBLING Program.

The repeat statement that Pascal provides is closely related to the while statement. The general form of the repeat statement is

repeat *statement* until *condition*

The general effect of executing the repeat statement is this. The statement is repeatedly executed until the condition becomes true. Specifically, the statement is first executed and then the condition is tested. If the condition is false, the statement is executed again, and the condition is tested again, until the condition finally becomes false.

The main computational portion of the program DOUBLING could have been rendered as follows:

```
repeat
   begin
      CURRENTVALUE := 2 * CURRENTVALUE ;
      YEAR := YEAR + 1
   end
until CURRENTVALUE >= GOALAMOUNT
```

Note that a repeat statement will always execute its *statement* part at least once; however, a while statement will not necessarily ever execute its statement part. Consequently, this formulation of the main part of the DOUBLING program assumes that initially CURRENTVALUE < GOALAMOUNT, while the original formulation does not make that assumption.

Note that in our sample repeat statement above, the begin . . . end pair is really unnecessary since the block of statements to be executed is clearly delineated by the repeat . . . until pair. For this reason, Pascal allows one to drop the begin . . . end "super-parentheses" around a compound statement when it is used as the *statement* of a repeat statement.

Exercises

Exercise 4-1   Write a program POWER that accepts two integers, BASE and EXP, as input and outputs the result of raising BASE to the power EXP.

Exercise 4-2   The factorial N! of the integer N is defined to be the product

$$1 * 2 * 3 * \ldots * (N-2) * (N-1) * N$$

Write a program FACT that accepts an integer N as input and outputs N!. Assuming that your program is correct, experiment with your computer to find out how large N must be before N! is too large for your computer to calculate.

Exercise 4-3   The *binomial coefficient* B(N,K) of two integers N and K is defined to be

$$B(N,K) = N! / (K! * (N-k)!)$$

[See Exercise 4.2.] Write a program BINOMIAL that accepts integers N and K as inputs and outputs B(N,K). Write your program using the definition of B(N,K) given above.

Exercise 4-4   Rewrite the program BINOMIAL in Exercise 4.3 to utilize the relations

$$B(N,0) = 1/N!$$

and

$$B(N+1,K+1) = [(N+1)/(K+1)] * B(N,K)$$

Compare the maximal sizes of N and K that the two versions of the program will accept before your computer encounters numbers too large for it to deal with.

Exercise 4-5   Write a program BRIDGE that accepts as input four integers SPADES, HEARTS, DIAMONDS, and CLUBS representing the numbers of the indicated kinds of cards to be found in a particular 13 card hand. The output of the program is to be the probability of being dealt such a hand. The theory of probability tells us that the odds of being dealt such a hand are

Z(SPADES,HEARTS,DIAMONDS,CLUBS) / B(52,13)

where

Z(A,B,C,D) = B(13,A) * B(13,B) * B(13,C) * B(13,D)

[See exercise 4.3.]

Exercise 4-6 Write a program TRIANGLE that accepts an integer HEIGHT as input and prints out a picture of the form

```
*
**
***
****
*****

   .
   .
   .
***  . . .  ***
```

with exactly HEIGHT lines. The figure is to be solidly filled in. [Hint: Use a for statement inside another for statement.]

Exercise 4-7 Write a modification of the program in problem Exercise 4-6 called TREE. This program also accepts an integer HEIGHT as input, but outputs a picture of the following form:

```
*
***
*****

  .
  .
  .
***  . . .  ***
```

Like TRIANGLE, this TREE is to have exactly HEIGHT lines and, of course, is to be solidly filled in.

Exercise 4-8 Write a program AVERAGE that will accept an indefinitely long sequence of positive real numbers as input. The sequence will be terminated by its last member being < 0. The program will output the number of reals that were input (not including the terminal 0), together with the average of these numbers. [Hint: Use a repeat statement.]

Exercise 4-9   Modify the program CHANGE in Chapter 2 so that instead of accepting only one line of input, it keeps up a loop in which it asks for input, outputs the value, asks for another line of input, outputs the value, and so on. The loop is to terminate when the value of the input line is < $0.00. Modify the program ANGLE in Chapter 3 in a similar manner. [Hint: Use a repeat statement.]

Exercise 4-10   The DOUBLING program is a special case of programs that compute growth and decay. The general form of a growth problem runs as follows. If the starting amount is A, starting quantity R is the growth rate, and P runs over the growth periods (years, months, days, and so forth), then at each succeeding period the CURRENTAMOUNT is given by

A,   A*(1+R),   A*(1+R)**2,   A*(1+R)**3,   . . .

where X**Y indicates X raised to the power Y. Note that the value at each period after the first is obtained by multiplying the preceding value by (1+R). For decay problems, a factor of (1-R) is used instead of (1+R). Write a program GROWTH that accepts three inputs: a STARTING-AMOUNT, a growth RATE, and a GOALAMOUNT. The output of the program is the number of periods (YEARS) that it will take for the STARTINGAMOUNT to reach or exceed the GOALAMOUNT at the given growth RATE.

Exercise 4-11   Economic models of societies consist of sets of equations relating such factors as total national INCOME, CONSUMER spending, private INVESTMENT, GOVERNMENT spending, and a host of other factors. For example, the following equations make up a very simple model of a Lilliputian economy:

```
INCOME(YEAR)
    = CONSUMER(YEAR)+INVESTMENT(YEAR)+GOVERNMENT(YEAR).
CONSUMER(YEAR)   = 0.4 * INCOME(YEAR-1).
INVESTMENT(YEAR) = 0.7 * (CONSUMER(YEAR)
                       - CONSUMER(YEAR-1)).
GOVERNMENT(YEAR) = 1000000 + 1000 * YEAR
```

Such models are used in simulation studies of economic behavior. Given knowledge of the necessary values in some starting YEAR (typically taken as YEAR = 0), one uses the equations to compute the values of the variables for successive years.

Write a program that will take two inputs: the initial value of INCOME for YEAR = 0 and a number SPAN of years. The output of the program should be a table of the values of the variables calculated over the SPAN using the equations of the model given above.

Chapter Five

Consultation & Diagnosis: Conditionals

The decision-making capabilities embodied in the while and repeat statements (Chapter 4) are fairly limited: we can decide whether or not to go on repeating the indicated operation. While this is clearly a powerful and important thing to do (if you don't make the decision, you'll go on forever), it does not allow us to control the flow of the conversation, that is, to switch between various alternative courses depending upon certain conditions. The capability to do this, embodied in the conditional and case statements, is the topic of this chapter. The topics here will include the following:

- Choosing different courses of action based on the truth or falsity of a condition.
- Using multiple conditional statements to carry out complex decision processes.
- Choosing among multiple alternatives based on the value of a certain variable or expression.

5.1   Decisions, Decisions

One of the basic types of human decision making is embodied in the assertion:

"If Blaise is healthy on Saturday, we'll picnic by the
Seine, otherwise we'll meet in his drawing room."

The essence of this sort of behavior is that based on the truth or falsity of a given condition (that Blaise is healthy on Saturday), we take alternative courses of action (either picnicking by the Seine or meeting in his drawing room). Pascal provides an almost direct translation of this sort of conversation in the *conditional* statement. Its general form is:

```
if condition then
    action 1
else
    action 2
```

Thus we could present our sample above as

```
if "Blaise is healthy on Saturday" then
    "we will picnic on the Seine"
else
    "we will meet in his drawing room"
```

In real Pascal programs, *condition* is any Boolean expression of the type we have already used in connection with while and repeat expressions. And the actions *action 1* and *action 2* are any acceptable Pascal statements. These may be simple assignment or READ or WRITE statements; or they may be compound begin-end statements, or repeat or while statements, or other conditional statements. Thus if YEAR, CURRENTVALUE, and GOALAMOUNT are declared as in the program DOUBLING, and if TRIPLE is a Boolean variable, then the following code fragment will have the effect of repeatedly tripling or doubling CURRENTVALUE until GOALAMOUNT is reached or exceeded:

```
if TRIPLE then
   while CURRENTVALUE < GOALAMOUNT do
   begin
      CURRENTVALUE := 3 * CURRENTVALUE;
      YEAR := YEAR + 1
   end
else
   while CURRENTVALUE < GOALAMOUNT do
   begin
      CURRENTVALUE := 2 * CURRENTVALUE;
      YEAR := YEAR + 1
   end
```

Pascal also accepts a short form of the conditional under which we only specify what to do if the condition is true, and nothing for the otherwise case. Its form is simply

if *condition* then *action*

Thus for example:

```
if "Blaise is healthy on Saturday" then
   "we will picnic on the Seine"
```

Let us note one important point of syntax here. The semicolon is used in Pascal as a *separator* of statements, not as a terminator of statements. This is important in the context of conditionals. For if one inadvertently adds a semicolon following action__1 in the full conditional, as in

if *condition* then
    action__1 ;
  else *action__2*

Pascal will attempt to interpret this as a short conditional

if *conditional* then *action__1*

followed by a dangling phrase

else *action__2*

which is meaningless, and total confusion will ensue. (The systems you are talking to are not smart enough to figure out what you meant. They only act on what you actually said.)

One other point of syntax is important to consider before we tackle a full program. This concerns the use of conditionals within conditionals. Let C1 and C2 be Boolean conditions, and let S1 and S2 be Pascal statements. Now consider the statement:

        if *C1* then if *C2* then *S1* else *S2*

There are two possible ways to group the parts of this so that it can be interpreted as a correct Pascal statement:

        if *C1* then [if *C2* then *S1* else *S2*]

and

        if *C1* then [if *C2* then *S1*] else *S2*

Pascal resolves this ambiguity by always choosing the first version.

    Let us now tackle a program to do a medical diagnosis. It will be prepared to deal with sick programmers having head or chest symptoms common in the winter months and will give them appropriate advice based on their symptoms. We will base it on the diagnostic procedures in *Take Care of Yourself: A Consumer's Guide to Medical Care*, by D.M. Vickery, M.D., and J.M. Fries, M.D., Addison-Wesley, 1976. Using Pascal's if . . . then . . . else conditionals combined with succinct natural language, we can express the basic diagnostic procedure as follows:

        if *Strong pain in ear* then
            See a physician today
        else if *Problem has lasted more than 14 days* then
            Make an appointment with a physician today
        else if *Sore throat is worst problem* then
            if [*Recent strep throat* or
                Rheumatic fever in the past or
                Nephritis in the past or
                Skin rash present] then
                See a physician today
            else if *Throat culture available* then
                    if *Throat culture is positive* then
                        Start antibiotic within 24 hours
                    else *Apply home treatment for sore throat*
            else if *Age < 25* then
                    See a physician today
            else if [*Temperature > 101* and *Pus in mouth*] then
                    See physician today
            else
                    Apply home treatment for sore throat
        else if *Fever has lasted more than 7 days* then
            Make an appointment with a physician today
        else
            Apply home treatment for colds.

There are at least two distinct ways to organize the program for advice. One would be to intermix the asking of questions, the application of the decision procedure, and the offering of advice. The other would be to clearly separate these three functions. The difficulty with the first alternative is that it would tend to produce an overly complex program. Since the second alternative avoids this pitfall, we select it. Thus the basic steps of the procedure are as follows:

1. Obtain the answers to the diagnostic questions.
2. Apply the decision procedure.
3. Output the advice.

This separation of functions implies that we will use variables to store the answers to the questions until we apply the decision procedure, and that we will also use variables to store the results of the decision procedure until we output the advice. Examination of the algorithm given shows that we will need a variable TEMPERATURE of type real, and variables PROBLEMDAYS, FEVERDAYS, and AGE of type integer. All the remaining questions can be answered with yes or no answers, and so we will use variables of type char to hold the characters Y or N.

There are undoubtedly many ways to store the results of the application of the algorithm. But one of the simplest is to use Boolean variables with appropriate names such as PHYSICIANTODAY. With these observations, we can present the first version or top level of the program MEDICALADVICE in Figure 5-1.

The process of obtaining the answers to the diagnostic questions is just a long sequence of WRITE and READ statements. The application of the decision procedure is virtually a transcription of the algorithm given above, simply replacing the natural language components with appropriate variables, Boolean expressions, or assignment statements. And the output of the advice is simply a sequence of conditional statements utilizing the Boolean variables and appropriate WRITE statements. The complete version of the program appears in Program 5-1.

```
program MEDICALADVICE(INPUT,OUTPUT);
(*  ------------------------------------------------------------  *
 *        This program provides diagnostic advice for a person    *
 *  suffering from a variety of common complaints.                *
 *        The input to the program consists of answers to a       *
 *  variety of questions about the user's state of health. These  *
 *  answers are either the characters Y or N, integer, or real.   *
 *        The output of the program is the medical advice to the  *
 *  poor suffering user.                                          *
 *  ------------------------------------------------------------  *)
    const
      YES = 'Y';
    var
      TEMPERATURE : real;

      PROBLEMDAYS, FEVERDAYS, AGE : integer;

      EARPAIN,         SORETHROAT,         RECENTSTREP,
      SKINRASH,        NEPHRITIS,          RHEUMATICFEV,
      CULTUREAVAIL,    CULTUREPOS,         PUSINMOUTH : char;

      PHYSICIANTODAY,  PHYSICIANAPPOINT,  ANTIBIOTIC,
      HOMETREATCOLD,   HOMETREATSORETHROAT : Boolean;

begin

    Obtain answers to all the diagnostic questions;

    Apply the decision procedure;

    Output the advice;

end.
```

Figure 5-1.   Outline of a Program for Medical Advice.

Program 5-1. A Program for Medical Advice

```
program MEDICALADVICE(INPUT,OUTPUT);
(* -------------------------------------------------------------- *
 *       This program provides diagnostic advice for a person    *
 * suffering from a variety of common complaints.                *
 *       The input to the program consists of answers to a       *
 * variety of questions about the user's state of health. These  *
 * answers are either the characters Y or N, integer, or real.   *
 *       The output of the program is the medical advice to the  *
 * poor suffering user.                                          *
 * -------------------------------------------------------------- *)
    const
       YES = 'Y';
    var
       TEMPERATURE : real;

       PROBLEMDAYS, FEVERDAYS, AGE : integer;

       EARPAIN,        SORETHROAT,      RECENTSTREP,
       SKINRASH,       NEPHRITIS,       RHEUMATICFEV,
       CULTUREAVAIL,   CULTUREPOS,      PUSINMOUTH : char;

       PHYSICIANTODAY, PHYSICIANAPPOINT, ANTIBIOTIC,
       HOMETREATCOLD,  HOMETREATSORETHROAT : Boolean;
begin
    WRITE('What is your age?');
    READ (AGE);
    WRITE('How many days have you had this problem?');
    READ (PROBLEMDAYS);
    WRITE('What is your temperature now?');
    READ (TEMPERATURE);
    WRITE('Do you have strong ear pain (Y or N)?');
    READ (EARPAIN);
    WRITE('Do you have a skin rash (Y or N)?');
    READ (SKINRASH);
    WRITE('Is a sore throat your worst problem (Y or N)?');
    READ (SORETHROAT);
    WRITE('Was a throat culture taken (Y or N)?');
    READ (CULTUREAVAIL);
    WRITE('Was it positive (Y or N)?');
    READ (CULTUREPOS);
    WRITE('Is there pus in the back of your mouth (Y or N)?');
    READ (PUSINMOUTH);
    WRITE('Have you recently had a strep throat (Y or N)?');
    READ (RECENTSTREP);
    WRITE('Have you had rheumatic fever in the past (Y or N)?');
    READ (RHEUMATICFEV);
    WRITE('Have you had nephritis in the past (Y or N)?');
    READ (NEPHRITIS);
```

Program 5-1. Continued.

```
if EARPAIN = YES then
   PHYSICIANTODAY    := TRUE
else if PROBLEMDAYS > 14 then
   PHYSICIANAPPOINT := TRUE
else if SORETHROAT = YES then
   if ((RECENTSTREP=YES) or (RHEUMATICFEV=YES) or
       (NEPHRITIS=YES) or (SKINRASH=YES)) then
       PHYSICIANTODAY := TRUE
   else if CULTUREAVAIL = YES then
       if CULTUREPOS = YES then
          ANTIBIOTIC := TRUE
       else
          HOMETREATSORETHROAT := TRUE
   else if AGE < 25 then
       PHYSICIANTODAY := TRUE
   else if ((TEMPERATURE > 101.0) and (PUSINMOUTH = YES)) then
       PHYSICIANTODAY := TRUE
   else
       HOMETREATSORETHROAT := TRUE
   end
else if FEVERDAYS > 7 then
   PHYSICIANAPPOINT := TRUE
else
   HOMETREATCOLD := TRUE;

WRITELN; WRITELN;
if PHYSICIANTODAY then
   WRITELN('Please see a physician today!')
else if PHYSICIANAPPOINT then
   WRITELN('Please make an appointment to see your physician.')
else if ANTIBIOTIC then
   WRITELN('Please start an antibiotic within 24 hours.')
else if HOMETREATSORETHROAT then
   begin
       WRITELN('Take 2 aspirin every 4 hours, gargle,');
       WRITELN('use a vaporizer, and quit smoking if you do.');
   end
else if HOMETREATCOLD then
   begin
       WRITELN('Take 2 aspirin, have a bowl of chicken soup,');
       WRITELN('rest, and call me in the morning.'          );
   end
else
   WRITELN('You''re healthy by your answers!  Back to work!');
end.
```

5.2   Multiple Alternatives

Occasions arise in which not only must multiple alternatives be considered, but these alternatives depend uniformly on the value of some variable. Now the method of nested if . . . then . . . else statements can be used to deal with this situation. However, Pascal provides an easier and more efficient means of expression for these problems. Consider a scheduling program at Blaise University. Among many other things, it must deal with the scheduling of the Babbage Memorial Lecture Hall in the LaPlace Engineering Building. Lectures at this university are serious affairs lasting three hours. (A lot of coffee is sold.) The courses in the engineering curriculum are relatively fixed, and in particular, the morning lectures in Babbage Hall have been fixed for years. Because of this, the scheduling program has these lectures written into it. Below is a portion of the type and variable declarations for this program:

```
type
    WEEK    = (SUN, MON, TUES, WED, THURS, FRI, SAT);
    COURSES = (COMPUTERS, AIRPLANES, CARS, ROCKETS,
               TELEVISION, STEREOS, MOTORCYCLES,...);

var
    DAY : WEEK;
    BABBAGE : COURSES
```

Then the following Pascal statement, known as a case statement, expresses the morning schedule for the auditorium:

```
case DAY of
      MON     : BABBAGE   := AIRPLANES;
      TUES    : BABBAGE   := COMPUTERS;
      WED     : BABBAGE   := TELEVISION;
      THURS   : BABBAGE   := CARS;
      FRI     : BABBAGE   := MOTORCYCLES;
      SAT,SUN : BABBAGE   := STEREOS
end  (* case *)
```

The general form of the case statement is:

```
case expression of
    labels : statement;
    labels : statement;

    labels : statement
end
```

Here the statements may be simple as in the preceding example, or they may be complex (for example, conditionals or compound statements). The expression is of some scalar type T other than real. The labels are elements of the type T. (Note that on each "arm" of the case, *labels* may be a single element of T or they may be several elements of T separated by commas.) The events which occur when such a statement is executed are as follows. First the *expression* is evaluated to obtain some value V belonging to type T. Then it is determined which statement corresponds to V (this determination is efficient) and that statement is executed.

Note that standard Pascal does not provide any "otherwise" label in case statements. In fact, the effect of a case statement in which the value of the expression does not match any of the labels is undefined and hence unpredictable. If it is important to utilize such an "otherwise" approach, nested conditionals must be applied. The following nested conditions are equivalent to the case example given above. Note that SAT and SUN are effectively treated as an "otherwise" case.

```
if DAY = MON then
   BABBAGE := AIRPLANES
else if DAY = TUES then
   BABBAGE := COMPUTERS
else if DAY = WED then
   BABBAGE := TELEVISION
else if DAY := THURS then
   BABBAGE := CARS
else if DAY := FRI then
   BABBAGE := MOTORCYCLES
else
   BABBAGE := STEREOS
```

Exercises

Exercise 5-1 Many people are confused about the need for tetanus shots. Below is an algorithm (taken from the Vickery and Fries book) for determining what should be done:

> if you have had ≥ 3 tetanus shots then
> if it is ≤ 5 years since last tetanus shot then
>   no shot needed
> else if the wound is clean and minor then
>   if it is < 10 years since last tetanus shot then
>   no shot needed
>   else see a physician today
> else see a physician today
> else see a physician today.

Write a program TETANUS that asks the user appropriate questions about his wound and gives him tetanus advice according to the algorithm above.

Exercise 5-2 The many students flooding into Blaise University need advice concerning the mathematics courses in which they should enroll. The requirements and recommendations are as follows:

> Major = English, Fine Arts, or Philosophy:
> No math required, but Logic 101 recommended.
> Major = Anthropology, Psychology, or Sociology:
> Statistics 101 required.
> Major = All others:
> Requirements depend on math SAT score:
> SAT < 450: Math 005–Remedial Algebra;
> SAT < 600: Math 101–Calculus I;
> SAT ≥ 700: Math 102–Calculus II;
> SAT ≥ 700: Math 103–Calculus III.

Write a program that will obtain the student's major and math SAT score as input and will output requirements and advice based on the preceding data. The output should be in a reasonable, "human" form.

Exercise 5-3 An integer is *prime* if no number evenly divides it other than 1 and itself. There are many occurrences of pairs of primes, such as 5 and 7, 11 and 13, 29 and 31, and so forth. Though extremely large pairs of primes have been found, no mathematician has been able to prove that there are infinitely many such pairs. Consider a program TWINPRIMES that accepts a positive integer BOUND as input and returns a list of all pairs of such twin primes less than or equal to the BOUND, together with the number of such pairs. Besides BOUND and COUNT, the program will need integer variables NUM and NUM2 to range over candidate pairs below BOUND. A top-level version of this program is given as follows:

```
program TWINPRIMES;
    var
        BOUND,COUNT,NUM,NUM2 : integer;
begin
    Input BOUND;
    Initialize COUNT,NUM, and NUM2;
    while NUM2 <= BOUND do
    begin

        Test NUM and NUM2 for primeness;

        if either NUM or NUM2 is not prime then
            Increment NUM and NUM2
        else
        begin
            Output NUM and NUM2;
            Increment NUM, NUM2, and COUNT;
        end;
    end; (* while *)

    Output final message;
end.
```

Add appropriate documentation and refine this to a complete program.

Exercise 5-4 Playing games is a universal human and computer activity. Writing the programs to play the games is even more fun. Here is an interesting board game that can be written using the machinery we have built up so far. The game is called QUEEN. The two players (in this case a human and a computer) alternate turns moving a single queen on a chessboard. The first one to move the queen into the lower left corner of the board wins. The human player goes first and gets to place the queen on any square on the top row or on the right-hand column.

Thus the input to the program is the initial position of the queen. The output is the sequence of moves made by the computer for its turns. [Hint: Number the board with coordinates as shown in Figure 5-2 below. Use two variables QROW and QCOL to hold the present coordinates of the queen. Note also that along the diagonals labeled SUMDIAGS, the sum of the row and column coordinates is constant, while along the diagonals labeled DIFFDIAGS, the difference of the row and column coordinates is constant. These facts can be used in the organization of diagonal moves.]

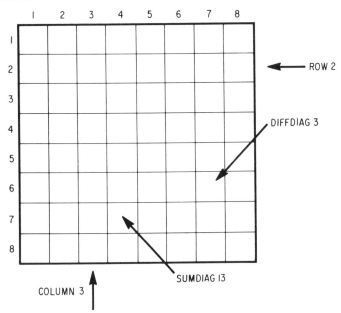

Figure 5-2. Labeling a Chessboard.

Exercise 5-5   Recall that a quadratic equation is an equation of the form:

$$ax^{**}2 + bx + c = 0.$$

The following rules cover the details of finding solutions, if any, for the equation.

1. If $a = 0$ and $b = 0$ and $c = 0$, the equation is true for all x.
2. If $a = 0$ and $b = 0$ and $c \neq 0$, the equation is never true.
3. If $a = 0$ and $b \neq 0$, there is one solution: $-c/b$.
4. If $a \neq 0$ and $c = 0$, there are two solutions: $-b/a$ and 0.
5. If $b^{**}2 - 4ac \gg 0$, there are two real roots given by:

$$\text{roots} = (-b \pm \text{sqrt}(b^{**}2 - 4ac))/2a.$$

6. Otherwise, there are two complex roots given by:

$$\text{roots} = (-b \pm \text{sqrt}(b^{**}2 - 4ac))/2a.$$

Write a program QUAD which will accept the three coefficients a,b, and c as input, and which will output the roots of the equation (with appropriate commentary) or gives appropriate informative messages.

Exercise 5-6

a) Show that any while statement can be rewritten using just repeat statements and conditional statements.

b) Similarly, show that any repeat statement can be rewritten using only while statements and conditional statements.

c) Show that any simple if-then statement can be rewritten using a while statement together with an additional BOOLEAN variable.

Chapter Six

Recording Conversations: I-O and Files

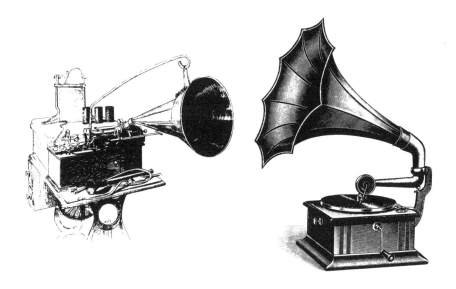

All of our conversations with the computer thus far have been casual in the sense that none of them referred to any previously stored information in the computer, and none of them made any permanent records in the computer for later use. We will remedy this situation now. The topics in this chapter will include the following:

■ Devices for recording and storing data.

■ Organization of data into files.

■ Utilization of files in Pascal programs.

■ Formatted input and output.

6.1   Recording Devices

Programs that run in interactive mode (as we have assumed all of ours do) usually get information and data from the user's terminal (for example, answers to questions and the like) and output data to the user's terminal (for example, medical advice). However, there are situations in which the same data must be used by the program during many different executions. It is tedious to reenter these data each time the program is run, especially if the data are at all extensive. There are also situations where it would be desirable to make the output of a program directly available either to itself at later executions or to other programs.

As we pointed out in Chapter 1, the computer's primary memory, the place where the program in fact resides when it is being executed, is a relatively scarce (and expensive) resource. Thus the storage of programs themselves between executions, as well as extra data for the programs' uses, must take place on secondary storage devices. These secondary storage devices (or *backing store*, as they are sometimes called) are slower in response time than the primary memory; however, relative to the cost per storable word, they are much cheaper than primary memory. Finally, and perhaps most importantly, they are permanent or long-term memory devices. When the machine is turned off (or someone pulls the plug), secondary memory retains what was stored in it. Primary memory is only short-term. When the power goes off, all traces of what was stored in it vanish. Thus data stored for multiple use by programs must be stored in secondary storage.

There are many different types of secondary storage devices. They vary considerably in cost, storage capacity, and speed of access. Most of them are electronic in form, such as magnetic drums, disks, tapes, and (recently) magnetic bubble memories. There are also nonmagnetic forms such as punched cards and punched paper tape. These non-magnetic forms are not only much slower than the electronic forms, but they are also slowly falling out of use. Therefore, we will ignore them in our discussion.

The most useful electronic device from the point of view of programs is the magnetic disk. (Magnetic drums and bubble memories are just as useful. However, the former are not seen very often, and the latter are just beginning to appear in computer systems.) In the environment of most present-day computer systems, it is possible to allow programs almost direct access to data that have been stored on magnetic disk. By contrast, it is much harder for programs to access data stored on magnetic tape. At installations where both disks and tape are available, the typical use of tape storage is for truly long-term memory. At times when the data on the tape will be needed by programs, it is copied from the tape onto the disks. When it is no longer immediately needed by programs, the tapes are updated (if necessary) by recopying the data on the disks back onto the tape and then erasing the data from the disks. (This procedure reflects the fact that at large time-sharing installations it is far cheaper to store data on tape than on disk. This is not quite so true with smaller personal computer systems.)

For these reasons, we will assume that all of our data storage is to take place on magnetic disks. Whether these are the large, expensive "hard" disks of large time-sharing systems or the smaller, cheaper "floppy" disks typically associated with mini- and microcomputers, the procedures for storing data will be the same.

6.2   Organizing Your Files

The amount of data that can be stored on magnetic disks is quite large. Consequently, one would expect that the disks will contain all sorts of different data to be used by different programs for different purposes. It therefore makes sense to view the disk as a large filing cabinet with the data broken up into separate files that can be dealt with independently. An individual file can be opened and looked through, or it can have data inserted into it.

Pascal provides such a conceptual apparatus. In fact, the apparatus Pascal provides makes no assumptions about the actual physical nature of the device on which the data in fact resides. It is almost as if it were by accident that the data are found on a physical device. (But a very fortunate accident indeed!)

What Pascal provides is a type of entity called a *file*. This is in fact our first example of a structured type in Pascal. A file is a complex object made up of uniform components of some other type. The components are organized into an ordered, open-ended sequence with a definite first element:

$$c1, \ c2, \ c3, \ . \ . \ .$$

For example, if we wish to utilize such a sequence of integers, we would begin by making the following type declaration:

```
type
   MYFILE = file of integer
```

Such a declaration, like the declaration of an enumeration type, causes the Pascal system to create means of manipulating a sequence of abstract entities. But there are two differences. First, in the enumeration type declaration, we state what entities belong to the sequence; in the file type declaration we do not. And second, the length of the sequence making up the enumeration type is fixed by its declaration; the length of the sequence making up the file type is not fixed by the declaration.

Well, if the file type declaration neither tells us what is in the list nor how long it is, what good is it? The answer is no good, without further machinery for putting things into the sequence or examining the sequence to see what might be there. The machinery that Pascal provides for this is the *file buffer variable*. In our example, the type declaration for MYFILE caused Pascal to automatically declare a very special integer variable, MYFILE^. This variable can be thought of as a window through which the elements of the sequence making up MYFILE can be viewed, or through which new elements may be added to the sequence.

At this point we must distinguish the two uses to which a file may be put. One use is for inputting information or data into the program from the outside world, and the other is for outputting information or data from the program to the outside world. If the file is to be used for input, then the file buffer variable (in our example, MYFILE^) is used as a window through which to view the components of MYFILE. And if the file is to be used for output, the file buffer variable is used as a window through which to put new elements into the sequence. Since computer systems are quite simpleminded, Pascal allows one to use a file only for input or only for output at any given point in the program. (One can switch the use in different places, but the consequences of such switches are serious.)

To tell Pascal that a given file is to be used for input, one uses the statement reset(. . .). Thus to tell Pascal that MYFILE is to be used for input, one would use the statement

    reset(MYFILE)

The corresponding instruction to use a file for output is the statement rewrite. Thus to instruct Pascal to use the file MYFILE for output, one would use the statement

    rewrite(MYFILE)

The window provided by the file buffer variable is capable of viewing exactly one element of the sequence at a time:

    $c_1, c_2, c_3, \ldots$

If the file MYFILE is going to be used as input and this is told to Pascal via the reset(MYFILE) statement, the Pascal file MYFILE is associated with a real external file (usually on the disk), the conceptual sequence of entities in MYFILE becomes the actual sequence of entities in the real external file, and the window or file buffer variable is positioned looking at the very first element of that sequence. We look through that window simply by accessing the buffer variable MYFILE^. Thus if NEXTVALUE is also an integer variable (recall that MYFILE is a file of integers), then

```
NEXTVALUE := MYFILE^
```

would assign the value in the window MYFILE^ to NEXTVALUE.

However, this action does not cause the value in the window MYFILE^ to change. (You will recall that accessing the value of a variable never changes the contents of the variable.) In order to change the value of the window, one must use the operator get(. . .) to move the window. The statement

```
get(MYFILE)
```

has the effect of advancing the window to the *next* element of the sequence, if there is one. (If there is no further element in the sequence, an error occurs.)

Consider the following code fragment, where TOTAL has been declared to be an integer variable:

```
TOTAL := MYFILE^;
repeat
   get(MYFILE);
   TOTAL := TOTAL + MYFILE^
until ????
```

If somehow we can find the right condition to substitute for ????, this fragment would have the effect of summing up all the elements of MYFILE. The difficulty is that we must have some way of terminating the repeat statement. The natural thing desired, of course, is to terminate exactly when we have reached the end of the real file sequence associated with the Pascal file MYFILE. The Pascal eof(. . .) statement provides exactly the required condition. As long as the file window MYFILE^ is *not* positioned at the physically last element of the actual file being input, eof(MYFILE) is false. But as soon as MYFILE^ is positioned at the physically last element of the real input file, eof(MYFILE) becomes true. Thus we may sum up the integers in MYFILE with

```
TOTAL := MYFILE^;
repeat
   get(MYFILE) ;
   TOTAL := TOTAL + MYFILE^
until eof(MYFILE)
```

Note that only two types of motion are possible for the file buffer variable: one step at a time forward via the use of get, or all the way back to the beginning at once via reset(. . .). Thus input files are strictly sequential: the data in them must be accessed in order starting from the beginning.

In a similar vein, the statement rewrite(MYFILE) not only instructs Pascal that MYFILE is to be used for output, but it also associates a clean or empty physical file with MYFILE and positions the window MYFILE^ at the start of this physical file. However, we do not access the buffer variable. Instead, we push values through the window by assigning them to the buffer variable. The effect of such assignments is to cause the value to be written onto the physical file at the current position of the buffer. Thus

```
MYFILE^ := 9
```

would cause 9 to be written into the file. Just as with input files, however, pushing a value through the window does not change the physical position of the window. Instead, this must be done using the operator put(. . .). Thus

```
MYFILE^ := 9 ;
put(MYFILE)
```

would have the effect of writing 9 into the file and then advancing the window to the next physical writing position. Note that for output files, the file sequence is regarded as completely open-ended, or potentially infinite. The window is always positioned looking at the last element of the file (if any) so that eof(MYFILE) is always true. But executing put(MYFILE) never causes an error (except by totally exhausting all available physical space on the disks.)

The following code (assuming INT has been declared to be an integer variable) will have the effect of writing the integers from 100 down to 1 into the physical file associated with MYFILE:

```
rewrite(MYFILE) ;
for INT := 100 downto 1 do
   begin
      MYFILE^ := INT ;
      put(MYFILE)
   end
```

Finally, we must note that all files declared and used in the program must be listed on the first line of the program following the name of the program. The entire group must be enclosed in parentheses with commas separating the individual file identifiers. Thus, for example, if MYFILE is declared as a file in the program HOARD, the initial line would appear as

```
program HOARD(MYFILE)
```

The means whereby a particular Pascal file (for example, MYFILE) comes to be associated with a particular real external file (such as a disk file) vary from computer system to computer system. In many interactive Pascal systems, before the system actually begins running the program, it will ask the user for the external names of the physical files to be associated with the Pascal files listed in the program line. Other systems allow one to add extra arguments to the reset or rewrite statements that specify the external files. Thus, for example, in one system, if there is a file with external name DATA.FIL, one uses the following to specify that it is to be connected to MYFILE in input mode:

```
reset(MYFILE,'DATA.FIL')
```

For more details, consult the manuals for your particular Pascal computer system.

We have discussed files of integers thus far, but Pascal does not restrict us to just these kinds of files. The general form of a file type declaration is

```
ident = {packed} file of type
```

Here *ident* of course is simply an identifier that will be the name of this particular file. And *type* is *any* acceptable Pascal *type*. Thus we may consider files of real, files of char, files of WEEK (given a previous declaration of the type WEEK), or files of any of the structured types we will introduce later. The expression

```
{packed}
```

in this declaration indicates that reserved word *packed* may or may not be present. If it is used, the system attempts to maintain the file in a means that is more conservative of primary memory than if it does not. Thus

```
METERREADINGS = file of real
```

and

```
SCRIBBLING = packed file of char
```

are both acceptable file type declarations.

Files of char (whether packed or unpacked) are the basis for legible input and output to Pascal programs. A special form of these files, called *textfiles*, is in fact structured into lines. The identifier *text* is a standard predeclared type that denotes textfiles. Thus

```
NOTES : text
```

is a valid declaration of NOTES as a textfile.

Standard Pascal provides two predeclared textfiles, INPUT and OUTPUT. If you use them, they should be listed in the program line, but they should not be reset or rewritten. This is automatically done by the Pascal system. In some Pascal systems they are automatically connected to external disk files. In others, they are connected to the terminal. Systems that automatically connect INPUT and OUTPUT to disk files usually provide some other predeclared file for input and output to the terminal. Often the same name (for example, TTY) is used both for the name of the input file from the terminal and for the output file to the terminal. (Lots of effort goes into making sure that the system sorts out what is what behind the scenes.) We will assume that this is indeed the situation in the rest of this chapter.

Now let us consider the following problem. We wish to construct a small program to act as a stenographer or notetaker. It will accept individual notes from the terminal and write them into a disk file, sequentially numbering each note. Let us agree that on input from the terminal, we will terminate each individual note with the # sign, and that we will terminate the entire sequence of notes with two # signs.

Obviously, we will need a textfile in our program for the output file; let us call it NOTES. The input file will be TTY, as we assumed above. We will also need an integer variable, such as NOTENUM, to keep track of the numbers associated with the notes. We can outline the program as in Figure 6-1.

```
Program NOTETAKER(TTY,NOTES);
(*  ---------------------------------------------------------- *
 *        This program enables the user to construct a file     *
 *  NOTES consisting of sequentially numbered notes.            *
 *        The input to the program is the notes typed in by     *
 *  the user. Each individual note is terminated by the         *
 *  symbol '#'. The entire sequence of notes is terminated      *
 *  by the symbols '##'.                                        *
 *        The output of the program is the file NOTES consisting *
 *  of the sequentially numbered notes.                         *
 *  ---------------------------------------------------------- *)
    var
       NOTES: TEXT;
       NOTENUM: integer;

begin

    Initialize NOTES and NOTENUM;

    while entire note sequence is not yet done do
       begin
           Write out current note number;

           Read next note over to output file NOTES;

           Start new line in output file NOTES and
                increment NOTENUM;

       end;
end.
```

Figure 6-1. Outline of a Notetaking Program.

Let us now begin refining this outline. The initialization of NOTES and NOTENUM is simple:

```
rewrite(NOTES);
NOTENUM := 1
```

Now consider the problem of reading the next note into the output file NOTES. Essentially, we keep examining the TTY window

TTYˆ, and as long as it is not the character #, we must write the value of TTYˆ over into NOTES and advance the TTY window. Now the value of TTYˆ can be written into NOTES by the following two statements:

```
NOTESˆ := TTYˆ;
put(NOTES)
```

Since the TTY window is advanced by get(TTY), the following compound statement carries out the work of writing the current value of the TTY window into NOTES and then advancing that window:

```
begin
   NOTESˆ:= TTYˆ;
   put(NOTES) ;
   get(TTY)
end
```

But we do this as long as the value in the TTY window is not the character #. Thus the process of reading the next note into NOTES is carried out by

```
while TTYˆ <> '#' do
   begin
      NOTESˆ := TTYˆ;
      put(NOTES) ;
      get(TTY)
   end
```

We must make one more observation. When this piece of code finishes execution, the TTY window will be looking at the final # that terminated the note just processed. Thus to genuinely complete processing of that note, we must follow this while statement with get(TTY) to advance the TTY window to the next character in the input file. This character will either be the first character of the next note or a second # terminating the entire session.

Thus our next refinement of the program NOTETAKER is presented in Figure 6-2.

```
program NOTETAKER(TTY,NOTES);
(*  ------------------------------------------------------------  *
*        This program enables the user to construct a file    *
*   NOTES consisting of sequentially numbered notes.          *
*        The input to the program is the notes typed in by    *
*   the user. Each individual note is terminated by the       *
*   symbol '#'. The entire sequence of notes is terminated    *
*   by the symbols '##'.                                      *
*        The output of the program is the file NOTES consisting *
*   of the sequentially numbered notes.                       *
*  ------------------------------------------------------------  *)
    var
        NOTES: TEXT;
        NOTENUM: integer;

begin
    rewrite(NOTES);
    NOTENUM := 1;

    while entire note sequence is not yet done do
        begin
            Write out current note number;
            while TTY^ <> '#' do
                begin
                    NOTES^ := TTY^;
                    put(NOTES);
                    get(TTY);
                end;  (* inner while *)

            get(TTY);

            Start new line in output file NOTES and
                increment NOTENUM;
        end;  (* outer while *)
end.
```

Figure 6-2. Refinement of the NOTETAKER Program.

Now we must make the final refinements. As we observed, when the inner while statement finishes executing, the TTY window is looking at the # symbol, which terminates the note just read. Consequently, after the get(TTY) following the inner while is executed, the TTY window must either be looking at the first character of the next note or it must be looking at the symbol #, this one being the second of two #'s in a row signaling the end of the session. Thus the required condition for the outer while is also simply that TTY be distinct from #: TTY^ <> '#'.

Now incrementing NOTENUM is easy: NOTENUM := NOTENUM+1. So this leaves us with only the problems of writing out the current note number and starting a new line in the file NOTES. Fortunately, this can be done using the WRITE and WRITELN procedures. Specifically,

```
writeln(NOTES)
```

will cause a new line to be started in the output file NOTES. And

```
write(NOTES,NOTENUM:2,'.      ')
```

will cause NOTENUM followed by a period and a tab to be written out in NOTES. (The literal in the WRITE statement contains a period followed by tab. We will discuss the use of WRITE, WRITELN, and READ in connection with textfiles more extensively later.) These observations now allow us to present the final program in Program 6-1.

```
program NOTETAKER(TTY,NOTES);
(*  ----------------------------------------------------------  *
 *        This program enables the user to construct a file     *
 *  NOTES consisting of sequentially numbered notes.            *
 *        The input to the program is the notes typed in by     *
 *  the user. Each individual note is terminated by the         *
 *  symbol '#'. The entire sequence of notes is terminated      *
 *  by the symbols '##'.                                        *
 *        The output of the program is the file NOTES consisting *
 *  of the sequentially numbered notes.                         *
 *  ----------------------------------------------------------  *)
     var
        NOTES: TEXT;
        NOTENUM: integer;

begin
     rewrite(NOTES);
     NOTENUM := 1;

     while TTY^ <> '#' do
        begin

            write(NOTES,NOTENUM:2,'.          ');
            while TTY^ <> '#' do
               begin
                  NOTES^ := TTY^;
                  put(NOTES);
                  get(TTY);
               end;  (* inner while *)

            get(TTY);
            writeln(NOTES);
            NOTENUM := NOTENUM + 1;
        end;  (* outer while *)
end.
```

Program 6-1. A Program for Taking NOTES.

6.3   Formatted I-O

Since textfiles are the basis for legible input and output between Pascal programs and the outside world, they are used for transferring both numerical and textual information. But textfiles by definition are files of type char, so how in the world can a Pascal program extract an integer from a textfile? The answer is that it can compute the number it *ought* to see. Thus if it sees the characters '5' and '2' in succession, it can compute that it just saw the number

$$5 * 10 + 2 * 1 = 52.$$

Of course, having to work out such things in everyday programs would be painful beyond belief, and so the Pascal systems provide ways of avoiding that work. Specifically, Pascal allows the procedures READ, WRITE, and WRITELN to be used with any textfile, just as we have used them earlier. The only change necessary is that we must specify the file that is to be handled. Thus

```
write(NOTES, 52, 'A little literal')
```

would cause the usual representation of the number 52 followed by the phrase

```
A little literal
```

to be written into the output file NOTES. WRITELN behaves similarly. Note that both of these procedures default to the standard predeclared file. They each check their first argument when called. If this argument is a file (being used hopefully for output), they write the appropriate information to this file. If their first argument is *not* a file, they write all the appropriate things to the standard file OUTPUT. Thus

```
write(52, 'A little literal')
```

is equivalent to

```
write(OUTPUT, 52, 'A little literal')
```

READ behaves analogously. If its first argument is a file, it tries to read the appropriate values from that file as an input file. Otherwise, it tries to read the appropriate things from the standard file INPUT. Thus

```
read(INFILE, NEXTINTEGER)
```

would try to read an integer from the file INFILE (provided everything had been appropriately declared).

As a simple illustration of the use of these facilities, Program 6-2 presents the program NOTETAKER using these procedures rather than file windows.

In fact, READ and WRITE can be defined in terms of file windows and the basic file procedures get and put. Thus the call read(INFILE, NEXTINTEGER) is equivalent to

```
NEXTINTEGER := INFILE^;
get(INFILE)
```

while write(OUTFILE,52) is equivalent to

```
OUTFILE^ := 52 ;
put(OUTFILE)
```

Finally, since textfiles are supposed to be broken into lines, Pascal provides a Boolean-valued operator EOLN(. . .) which recognizes the ends of lines. Thus if NOTES is a textfile, EOLN(NOTES) is true if and only if the file window NOTES^ is positioned at the end of a line. The expression EOLN alone is synonymous with EOLN(INPUT).

```
program NOTETAKER(TTY,NOTES);
(* --------------------------------------------------------------- *
 *        This program enables the user to construct a file        *
 * NOTES consisting of sequentially numbered notes.                *
 *        The input to the program is the notes typed in by        *
 * the user. Each individual note is terminated by the             *
 * symbol '#'. The entire sequence of notes is terminated          *
 * by the symbols '##'.                                            *
 *        The output of the program is the file NOTES consisting   *
 * of the sequentially numbered notes.                             *
 * --------------------------------------------------------------- *)
    var
        CH : char;
        NOTES: TEXT;
        NOTENUM: integer;

begin
    rewrite(NOTES);
    NOTENUM := 1;
    read(TTY,CH);

    while CH <> '#' do
        begin

            write(NOTES,NOTENUM:2,'.        ');
            while CH <> '#' do
                begin
                    write(NOTES,CH);
                    read(TTY,CH);
                end;  (* inner while *)

            read(TTY,CH);
            writeln(NOTES);
            NOTENUM := NOTENUM + 1;
        end;  (* outer while *)
end.
```

Program 6-2. A Revised Version of NOTETAKER.

Exercises

Exercise 6-1 Write a program STATISTICS which believes that the file SCORES consists of INTEGERs, and which reads through the file, computing the mean and the standard deviation of the entries. Given k numbers N1, . . . ,Nk, their mean M is given by

$$M = (N1 + N2 + . . . + Nk) / k,$$

and their standard deviation S is given by

$$S = SQRT[[(N1**2 + N2**2 + . . . + Nk**2) - 2*(M**2))] / (k-1)].$$

Exercise 6-2 Let OLDSCORES and NEWSCORES be two files of real numbers, each of which has been sorted in ascending order. Write a program MERGE which takes these two files as input, and produces as output a third file MERGEDSCORES which is made up of the entries from OLDSCORES and NEWSCORES merged together in one sorted file.

Exercise 6-3 Write a program SUBSTITUTE which takes a TEXTFILE OLDTEXT as input togther with a pair of CHARacters OLDCHAR and NEWCHAR which are read in from the terminal. The output of the program is to be a file NEWTEXT which is identical with OLDTEXT except that all instances of OLDCHAR have been replaced by NEWCHAR.

Chapter Seven

Table Talk: Arrays

Sophisticated talk has always found its place at the table, but we will do this one better: our first sophisticated talk will be about tables! Not only are tables excellent places at that to eat and talk, but they also make powerful programming tools. The mechanism which Pascal provides for the representation of tables is the *array variable*. The topics in this chapter are the following:

- The nature of array variables.
- The use of array variables to represent simple tables.
- The use of array variables to construct higher dimensional tables.

7.1 Listing Your Points

Much of the information we deal with in our world is arranged in the form of tables such as the calorie table below:

Food	Calorie Value
Milk	159
Broccoli	100
.	.
.	.
.	.
Bacon	10

For convenience, we have omitted the portion size from this table.

Pascal's mechanism for dealing with tables is the *array variable.* This can be thought of as a simple table of individual variables. For example, suppose we have defined a type called FOODS, and we want to deal with the calorie table given above. As with everything else in Pascal, we must give our table or list its own name; suppose we choose ENERGYVALUE. Of course, choosing this name ourselves doesn't tell Pascal a thing about it. To instruct Pascal in what we desire, we use a variable declaration:

```
var
    ENERGYVALUE: array [FOODS] of integer;
```

The reserved word *array*, of course, tells Pascal that we are declaring an array variable. The bracketed expression

```
[FOODS]
```

describes the indices that are to be used for the table. And the expression following the reserved word of must be the name of a type: each of the variables in this table will be of this type. Here the word integer following of indicates that each variable in the list is to be of type integer.

The general form of an array variable declaration is:

```
var
    identifier: array [ indices ] of type
```

Identifier naturally is the name we choose to use for the array. *Indices* is the name of a type we are going to use as the indices for the table. It must be a scalar type other than real. And finally, *type* is the name of the type that each of the variables in the table will be prepared to contain.

Once we have specified an array to Pascal, we must be able to refer to the individual variables of which it is composed. We do this by suffixing the array name with the index enclosed in square brackets. Thus, if BACON and EGGS are both elements of the enumeration type FOODS, we may refer to the variables of the table ENERGYVALUE as

ENERGYVALUE[BACON]

and

ENERGYVALUE[EGGS]

Though the names for these variables are complex, they are still individual variables of the type indicated in the declaration. Thus we may assign appropriate values to them, and we may read values out of them. Consequently, if CALORIES is an integer variable, the following are all meaningful Pascal statements:

ENERGYVALUE[BACON] := 10

ENERGYVALUE[EGGS] := 30

CALORIES := (2 * ENERGYVALUE[EGGS])
            + (3 * ENERGYVALUE[BACON])

The expression between square brackets used for the index may be a constant as above, or it may be a variable as in

ENERGYVALUE[DISH]

where DISH is a variable of type FOODS. Finally, the index expression may even be a complex expression involving operators, as in

ENERGYVALUE[pred(BACON)]

Now let us consider the construction of a dieter's breakfast program. It will aid the poor dieter by accepting his or her description of the meal about to be consumed and reporting the calorie value of that meal. Arrays are a natural structure to use in such a program since we expect to store the calorie values of standard portions of various foods. Of course, we will have to explicitly store these values into the array in the program. The overall structure of the program will be as shown in Figure 7-1.

```
program DIET(INPUT,OUTPUT);
(*  --------------------------------------------------------------  *
    *        This program allows the user to calculate the calorie  *
    *  value of a breakfast made up of common foods. The user inputs *
    *  a description (on one line) of a meal in terms of serving     *
    *  descriptions of various items making up her or his meal.      *
    *        A serving description consists of a food followed by a  *
    *  number indicating the number of servings of that food, as     *
    *  for example:                                                  *
    *                                                                *
    *        Cantaloupe 1  Egg 2  Bacon 2  Coffee 1  Cream 1         *
    *                                                                *
    *        The output of the program is the calorie value of       *
    *  the meal.                                                      *
    *  --------------------------------------------------------------  *)
begin

    Initialize the array variable;

    Output instructions to the user;

    Input specification of meal and compute total calories;

    Output calorie value to user;

end.
```

Figure 7-1. A Program for Dieting Assistance.

Now consider the data structures we will need. Perhaps the most natural way to proceed would be to define a type FOOD such as

```
FOODS = (GRAPEFRUIT, CANTALOUPE, . . . );
```

and then define an array such as ENERGYVALUE as we did above. Conceptually, this would be an excellent way of proceeding. Although standard Pascal does not allow direct input or output of enumeration types, we will write our first version pretending that it does. This will allow us to construct a very attractive program. Later we will force it into the mold required by standard Pascal. (As we will see, not allowing input and output of enumeration types is a severe and stupid restriction. Some Pascal systems have extensions allowing it. By all means use it when you can!)

Now consider the variables necessary in our program. We will need an array ENERGYVALUE to hold the calorie values thus:

```
ENERGYVALUE : array [FOODS] of integer
```

We will also need integer variables NUMSERVINGS and CALORIES and a variable ITEM ranging over the type FOODS:

```
ITEM: FOODS;
NUMSERVINGS, CALORIES: integer;
```

The central part of the program — reading in the meal specification and computing the caloric value of the meal – can now be carried out by the following Pascal code:

```
CALORIES    := 0;
NUMSERVINGS := 0;

READLN;
while not(EOLN) do
begin
   READ(ITEM,NUMSERVINGS);
   CALORIES := CALORIES
             + (NUMSERVINGS * ENERGYVALUE[ITEM])
end;
```

Thus our program has been refined to the stage that appears in Figure 7-2.

```
program DIET(INPUT,OUTPUT);
(*  --------------------------------------------------------------  *
 *        This program allows the user to calculate the calorie    *
 *  value of a breakfast made up of common foods. The user inputs  *
 *  a description (on one line) of a meal in terms of serving      *
 *  descriptions of various items making up her or his meal.       *
 *        A serving description consists of a food followed by     *
 *  a number indicating the number of servings of that food, as    *
 *  for example:                                                   *
 *                                                                 *
 *        Cantaloupe 1  Egg 2  Bacon 2  Coffee 1  Cream 1          *
 *                                                                 *
 *        The output of the program is the calorie value of        *
 *  the meal.                                                      *
 *  --------------------------------------------------------------  *)
    type
      FOODS =
        (GRAPEFRUIT,   CANTALOUPE,   BANANA,    TOMATOJUICE,
         ORANGEJUICE,  MILK,         TOAST,     BISCUIT,
         MUFFIN,       BUTTER,       OATMEAL,   DRYCEREAL,
         CREAM,        SUGAR,        COFFEE,    CHEESE,
         EGG,          SAUSAGE,      BACON                 );
      ENERGYVALUE: array [FOODS] of integer;
      ITEM: FOODS;
      NUMSERVINGS,CALORIES: integer;

begin
    Initialize the array variable;
    Output instructions to the user;

    CALORIES    := 0;
    NUMSERVINGS := 0;

    (* Input the specification *)
    READLN;
    while not(EOLN) do
    begin
      READ(ITEM,NUMSERVINGS);
      CALORIES  := CALORIES +
                      (NUMSERVINGS * ENERGYVALUE[ITEM]);
    end;
    Output calorie value to user;
end.
```

Figure 7-2. Refinement of the Diet Program.

To print out the menu, a simple for statement will do the trick:

```
for ITEM := GRAPEFRUIT to BACON do
    WRITELN(ITEM, '. . .', ENERGYVALUE[ITEM]:3,' CALORIES')
```

The initialization of the array ENERGYVALUE is simply a matter of assigning the correct calorie value to each component variable. And of course output is easy. Thus our final program now appears as given in Program 7-1.

Program 7-1. The DIET Advice Program

```
program DIET(INPUT,OUTPUT);
(*  ----------------------------------------------------------  *
*        This program allows the user to calculate the calorie   *
*   value of a breakfast made up of common foods. The user inputs *
*   a description (on one line) of a meal in terms of serving     *
*   descriptions of various items making up her or his meal.      *
*        A serving description consists of a food followed by     *
*   a number indicating the number of servings of that food, as   *
*   for example:                                                  *
*                                                                *
*        Cantaloupe 1  Egg 2  Bacon 2  Coffee 1  Cream 1          *
*                                                                *
*        The output of the program is the calorie value of        *
*   the meal.                                                      *
*  ----------------------------------------------------------  *)
    type
        FOODS =
            (GRAPEFRUIT,  CANTALOUPE,   BANANA,    TOMATOJUICE,
             ORANGEJUICE, MILK,         TOAST,     BISCUIT,
             MUFFIN,      BUTTER,       OATMEAL,   DRYCEREAL,
             CREAM,       SUGAR,        COFFEE,    CHEESE,
             EGG,         SAUSAGE,      BACON                  );
    var
        ENERGYVALUE: array [FOODS] of integer;
        ITEM: FOODS;
        NUMSERVINGS,CALORIES: integer;
```

Program 7-1. Continued.

```
begin
   (* Initialize variables *)
   ENERGYVALUE[MILK]            := 159;
   ENERGYVALUE[BANANA]          :=  50;
   ENERGYVALUE[CANTALOUPE]      := 150;
   ENERGYVALUE[TOMATOJUICE]     := 100;
   ENERGYVALUE[GRAPEFRUIT]      := 100;
   ENERGYVALUE[ORANGEJUICE]     := 100;
   ENERGYVALUE[TOAST]           :=  25;
   ENERGYVALUE[BISCUIT]         :=  35;
   ENERGYVALUE[MUFFIN]          :=  40;
   ENERGYVALUE[DRYCEREAL]       :=  20;
   ENERGYVALUE[OATMEAL]         := 100;
   ENERGYVALUE[BUTTER]          :=   5;
   ENERGYVALUE[CREAM]           :=  30;
   ENERGYVALUE[COFFEE]          :=   0;
   ENERGYVALUE[SUGAR]           :=   4;
   ENERGYVALUE[CHEESE]          :=  30;
   ENERGYVALUE[EGG]             :=  50;
   ENERGYVALUE[BACON]           :=  10;
   ENERGYVALUE[SAUSAGE]         :=  60;
   (* Display Menu *)
   WRITELN( 'Breakfast Menu:');
   WRITELN( '============== ');
   for ITEM := GRAPEFRUIT to BACON do
   WRITELN( ITEM ,'...', ENERGYVALUE[ITEM]:3,' CALORIES');
   WRITELN;
   WRITELN( 'Please input your meal specification');
   CALORIES := 0;
   NUMSERVINGS := 0;

   (* Input the specification *)
   READLN;
   while not(EOLN) do
   begin
      READ(ITEM,NUMSERVINGS);
      CALORIES := CALORIES +
                  (NUMSERVINGS * ENERGYVALUE[ITEM]);
   end;
   WRITELN;
   WRITELN('The energy value of this meal is',
           CALORIES:5,    ' calories.'    );

end.
```

Here is a sample execution of this program on a DEC PDP10 computer:

```
BREAKFAST MENU:
================
GRAPEFRUIT. . .100 CALORIES
CANTALOUPE. . .150 CALORIES
    BANANA. . . 50 CALORIES
TOMATOJUIC. . .100 CALORIES
ORANGEJUIC. . .100 CALORIES
      MILK. . .159 CALORIES
     TOAST. . . 25 CALORIES
   BISCUIT. . . 35 CALORIES
    MUFFIN. . . 40 CALORIES
    BUTTER. . .  5 CALORIES
   OATMEAL. . .100 CALORIES
 DRYCEREAL. . . 20 CALORIES
     CREAM. . . 30 CALORIES
     SUGAR. . .  4 CALORIES
    COFFEE. . .  0 CALORIES
    CHEESE. . . 30 CALORIES
       EGG. . . 50 CALORIES
   SAUSAGE. . . 60 CALORIES
     BACON. . . 10 CALORIES
PLEASE INPUT YOUR MEAL SPECIFICATION
grapefruit 1 coffee 1 cream 1 toast 2 butter 1 egg 2 sausage 3
THE ENERGY VALUE OF THIS MEAL IS  465 CALORIES.
EXIT
```

7.2 Speaking Literally

Any dieter would be depressed by a menu that listed the calories of each and every item. It would be kind if we could replace the calorie statement in our menu listing with a description of the servings (½ grapefruit and so forth). Presumably what we need is a table

```
DESCRIPTION: array [ FOODS ] of ??
```

The question is what sort of type ?? could we use? What we want is something like the literal we have used in WRITE statements to output descriptive messages. However, we have never said that there was a type consisting of literals, and so it would not be possible to define an array of literals. Fortunately, this problem has an easy solution. Literals are not treated as a separate type because they are just arrays of char. Thus the literal

```
'The slithy toves did gyre'
```

is really just an array of 25 characters.

Now before we can continue talking about arrays of characters, we must discuss the problem of using integer indices in arrays. The general form of an array declaration,

```
array [ base-type ] of type
```

requires that the indices actually constitute a type. So if we want to use integers for indices, it would seem that our only choice is:

```
array[ integer ] of type
```

This makes a very big array! For our small sentence above we only need 25 entries. However, this would give us an effectively infinite array! One solution would be to try to define an enumeration type consisting of just the numbers we need:

```
ONETO25 = (1,2,3,4,5,6,7,8,9,10,11,12,
           13,14,15,16,17,18,19,20,21,22,23,24,25);
```

Although Pascal will not let us speak in just this way, it does allow an idiom that is equivalent. Namely, it will let us use the expression

```
1..25
```

for exactly this collection of numbers. That is, for all intents and purposes, the expression $1..25$ can be taken as if we were allowed the definition

```
1..25 = (1,2,3,4,5,6,7,8,9,10,11,12,
         13,14,15,16,17,18,19,20,21,22,23,24,25);
```

This is an example of the description of a *subrange* type. As the name suggests, subrange types are subsidiary portions of larger parent types. These parent types must be enumerated types such as integer, char, or a user-defined enumeration type. In fact, they may be any scalar type other than real. The parent type in our example is type integer.

A subrange type description is an expression of the form

A..B

where A and B are elements of the parent type. Relative to the built-in ordering of this parent type, A must occur before B. The elements of the type are all the elements of the parent type lying between A and B, inclusive. Thus relative to the parent type CHAR,

LETTER = 'A'..'Z'

is the subrange type consisting of the upper case letters from the type CHAR.

Returning to our earlier example,

'The slithy toves did gyre'

is therefore a packed array[1..25] of char. (You will recall that the adjective "packed" simply indicates that Pascal attempts to use a very compact internal representation of the object – in this case, the array.) While there is no single type of all literals, we can declare a type of literals of any fixed length, since this is just the packed array [1..THATLENGTH] of char type.

Thus we may declare or define the type

STRING = packed array[1..STRINGSIZE] of CHAR

where STRINGSIZE is treated as a constant. If in fact STRINGSIZE = 25, then

'The slithy toves did gyre'

would be a constant of type STRING.

As with all types, we may declare variables over such types, assign values to them, and so forth. Thus, given that SENTENCE was declared to be of type STRING, the following is an acceptable Pascal statement:

SENTENCE := 'The slithy toves did gyre'

And in fact, after this assignment, it would be the case that SENTENCE[10] would be equal to 'y'.

Now given the definition

```
STRING = packed array[ 1..25 ] of CHAR;
```

we may declare

```
DESCRIPTION: array[ FOODS ] of STRING;
```

Then after assigning appropriate literals to each of the variables, we can print out the new version of the menu with

```
for ITEM := GRAPEFRUIT to BACON do
WRITELN(ITEM, '...', DESCRIPTION[ITEM] )
```

Consequently, we may revise the program DIET, as shown in Program 7-2.

Using a DEC PDP10 computer again, a sample execution of this version appears:

```
BREAKFAST MENU:
===============
GRAPEFRUIT. . .ONE-HALF, FRESH PINK
CANTALOUPE. . .ONE-HALF, SUPER JUICY
    BANANA. . .BAHAMIAN, SLICED
TOMATOJUIC. . .ONE-HALF CUP, PA'S OWN
ORANGEJUIC. . .ONE-HALF CUP(SUPER FRESH)
      MILK. . .ONE CUP, FRESH AND CREAMY
     TOAST. . .ONE SLICE, UNBUTTERED
   BISCUIT. . .FRESH-BAKED, BUTTERMILK
    MUFFIN. . .NATURAL BRAN AND CORN
    BUTTER. . .ONE PAT, CREAMERY FRESH
   OATMEAL. . .STEEL-CUT, OLD-FASHIONED
  DRYCEREAL. . .GRANOLA OR WHEATIES
     CREAM. . .2 TABLESPOONS, LIGHT
     SUGAR. . .ONE TEASPOON GRANULATED
    COFFEE. . .BLACK & STRONG: WAKE-UP
    CHEESE. . .MONTEREY JACK, 1 SLICE
       EGG. . .ONE LARGE FRESH-LAID
   SAUSAGE. . .ONE OF MA'S OWN
     BACON. . .ONE THICK-CUT SLICE
PLEASE INPUT YOUR MEAL SPECIFICATION
banana 1 cream 2 sugar 1 muffin 1 coffee 1
THE ENERGY VALUE OF THIS MEAL IS  104 CALORIES.
EXIT
```

Program 7-2. The Program DIET
with DESCRIPTIONS of FOODS Added.

```
program DIET(INPUT,OUTPUT);
(*  ------------------------------------------------------------  *
 *        This program allows the user to calculate the calorie  *
 *   value of a breakfast made up of common foods. The user inputs  *
 *   a description (on one line) of a meal in terms of serving  *
 *   descriptions of various items making up her or his meal.  *
 *        A serving description consists of a food followed by  *
 *   a number indicating the number of servings of that food, as  *
 *   for example:  *
 *  *
 *        Cantaloupe 1   Egg 2   Bacon 2   Coffee 1   Cream 1  *
 *  *
 *        The output of the program is the calorie value of  *
 *   the meal.  *
 *  ------------------------------------------------------------  *)
    const
       STRINGSIZE = 25;
    type
       FOODS =
          (GRAPEFRUIT,   CANTALOUPE,   BANANA,    TOMATOJUICE,
           ORANGEJUICE,  MILK,         TOAST,     BISCUIT,
           MUFFIN,       BUTTER,       OATMEAL,   DRYCEREAL,
           CREAM,        SUGAR,        COFFEE,    CHEESE,
           EGG,          SAUSAGE,      BACON                 );
       STRING = packed array [ 1..STRINGSIZE ] of CHAR;
    var
       ENERGYVALUE: array [FOODS] of integer;
       DESCRIPTION: array[ FOODS ] of STRING;
       ITEM: FOODS;
       NUMSERVINGS,CALORIES: integer;
begin
    (* Initialize variables *)
    ENERGYVALUE[MILK]               := 159;
    ENERGYVALUE[BANANA]             := 50;
    ENERGYVALUE[CANTALOUPE]         := 150;
    ENERGYVALUE[TOMATOJUICE]        := 100;
    ENERGYVALUE[GRAPEFRUIT]         := 100;
    ENERGYVALUE[ORANGEJUICE]        := 100;
    ENERGYVALUE[TOAST]              := 25;
    ENERGYVALUE[BISCUIT]            := 35;
    ENERGYVALUE[MUFFIN]             := 40;
    ENERGYVALUE[DRYCEREAL]          := 20;
    ENERGYVALUE[OATMEAL]            := 100;
    ENERGYVALUE[BUTTER]             := 5;
    ENERGYVALUE[CREAM]              := 30;
    ENERGYVALUE[COFFEE]             := 0;
```

Program 7-2. Continued.

```
ENERGYVALUE[SUGAR]              :=    4;
ENERGYVALUE[CHEESE]             :=   30;
ENERGYVALUE[EGG]                :=   50;
ENERGYVALUE[BACON]              :=   10;
ENERGYVALUE[SAUSAGE]            :=   60;

DESCRIPTION[MILK]          := 'One cup, fresh and creamy';
DESCRIPTION[BANANA]        := 'Bahamian, sliced          ';
DESCRIPTION[CANTALOUPE]    := 'One-half, super juicy     ';
DESCRIPTION[TOMATOJUICE]   := 'One-half cup, Pa''s own   ';
DESCRIPTION[GRAPEFRUIT]    := 'One-half fresh pink       ';
DESCRIPTION[ORANGEJUICE]   := 'One-half cup(super fresh)';
DESCRIPTION[TOAST]         := 'One slice, unbuttered     ';
DESCRIPTION[BISCUIT]       := 'Fresh-baked, buttermilk   ';
DESCRIPTION[MUFFIN]        := 'Natural bran and corn     ';
DESCRIPTION[DRYCEREAL]     := 'Granola or Wheaties       ';
DESCRIPTION[OATMEAL]       := 'Steel-cut, old-fashioned  ';
DESCRIPTION[BUTTER]        := 'One pat, creamery fresh   ';
DESCRIPTION[CREAM]         := '2 tablespoons, light      ';
DESCRIPTION[COFFEE]        := 'Black & strong: wake-up   ';
DESCRIPTION[SUGAR]         := 'One teaspoon granulated   ';
DESCRIPTION[CHEESE]        := 'Monterey Jack, 1 slice    ';
DESCRIPTION[EGG]           := 'One large fresh-laid      ';
DESCRIPTION[BACON]         := 'One thick-cut slice       ';
DESCRIPTION[SAUSAGE]       := 'One of Ma''s own          ';

(* Display Menu *)
WRITELN( 'Breakfast Menu:');
WRITELN( '============== ').
for ITEM := GRAPEFRUIT to BACON do
   WRITELN( ITEM ,'...', DESCRIPTION[ITEM]);
WRITELN;
WRITELN( 'Please input your meal specification');
CALORIES := 0;
NUMSERVINGS := 0;
(* Input the specification *)
READLN;
while not(EOLN) do
   begin
   READ(ITEM,NUMSERVINGS);
   CALORIES  := CALORIES
             + (NUMSERVINGS * ENERGYVALUE[ITEM]);
   end;
WRITELN;
WRITELN('The energy value of this meal is',
      CALORIES:5,        ' calories.'    );
end.
```

Finally, we must face up to the ugly fact that standard Pascal does not permit input or output of enumeration types. (So much the poorer for standard Pascal!) So to get around this we must apply the gruesome device of coding the food items by numbers. When we do this, our use of the enumeration type FOODS in this program becomes superfluous, and so we will drop it. Instead, we make the codes for the foods the fundamental things we manipulate. Our first step toward the new version of DIET is outlined in Figure 7-3.

```
program DIET(INPUT,OUTPUT);
(*  ----------------------------------------------------------  *
 *          This program allows the user to calculate the calorie  *
 *  value of a breakfast made up of common foods. The user inputs  *
 *  a description of a meal in terms of serving descriptions of  *
 *  various items making up her or his meal.                  *
 *          A serving description consists of a food code (given  *
 *  by the menu) followed by a number indicating the number of  *
 *  servings of that food. A sample input line would be:       *
 *                                                            *
 *              1 2    13 4    9 5    0 0                      *
 *  The sequence of serving description terminates with a       *
 *  description of item 0 (any number of servings will do).    *
 *          The output of the program is the calorie value of   *
 *  the meal.                                                  *
 *  ----------------------------------------------------------  *)
begin

    Initialize the array variables;

    Output instructions to the user;

    Input specification of meal and compute total calories;

    Output calorie value to user;

end.
```

Figure 7-3. A Program for Dieting Assistance.

Now let us determine the necessary data structures. First, count the number of foods (19, as it turns out), and let MAXFOOD be a constant with this value

```
MAXFOOD = 19;
```

Then let FOODCODES be the subrange type

```
FOODCODES = 1..MAXFOOD;
```

Next we will declare the array ENERGYVALUES to hold the calorie values:

```
ENERGYVALUE: array [FOODCODES] of integer;
```

Now let NUMSERVINGS and CALORIES be declared as integer variables, and let ITEM range over a subrange of type integer:

```
ITEM: 1..MAXFOOD;
```

For the sake of variety, we will change the central part of the program to read as follows:

```
CALORIES    := 0;
ITEM        := 1;
NUMSERVINGS := 0;

repeat
   CALORIES := CALORIES
                 + (NUMSERVINGS * ENERGYVALUE[ITEM]);
   READ(ITEM,NUMSERVINGS)
until ITEM = 0
```

Thus our program has been refined to the stage that appears in Figure 7-4.

And finally, we must introduce an array of literals to name and describe the food items. Let us use the type STRING as we did before. Then we may declare

```
FOODNAME: array[ FOODCODES ] of STRING ;
```

The final version of this program now appears in Program 7-3.

```
program DIET(INPUT,OUTPUT);
(*  ------------------------------------------------------------- *
 *         This program allows the user to calculate the calorie  *
 *  value of a breakfast made up of common foods. The user inputs *
 *  a description of a meal in terms of serving descriptions of   *
 *  various items making up her or his meal.                      *
 *         A serving description consists of a food code (given   *
 *  by the menu) followed by a number indicating the number of    *
 *  servings of that food. A sample input line would be:          *
 *                                                                *
 *                    1 2   13 4   9 5   0 0                       *
 *                                                                *
 *  The sequence of serving description terminates with a         *
 *  description of item 0 (any number of servings will do).       *
 *         The output of the program is the calorie value of      *
 *  the meal.                                                      *
 *  ------------------------------------------------------------- *)
    const
       MAXFOOD    = 19;
    type
       FOODCODES = 1..MAXFOOD;
    var
       ENERGYVALUE: array [FOODCODES] of integer;
       ITEM: 0..MAXFOOD;
       NUMSERVINGS,CALORIES: integer;

begin
   Initialize the array variables;
   Output instructions to the user;

   CALORIES    := 0;
   ITEM        := 1;
   NUMSERVINGS := 0;

   (* Input the specification *)
   repeat
      CALORIES := CALORIES
                    + (NUMSERVINGS * ENERGYVALUE[ITEM]);
      READ(ITEM,NUMSERVINGS);
   until ITEM = 0;

   Output calorie value to user;
end.
```

Figure 7-4.   Refinement of the Diet Program.

```
program DIET(INPUT,OUTPUT);
(*  ------------------------------------------------------------  *
 *        This program allows the user to calculate the calorie   *
 *   value of a breakfast made up of common foods. The user inputs *
 *   a description of a meal in terms of serving descriptions of   *
 *   various items making up her or his meal.                      *
 *        A serving description consists of a food code (given     *
 *   by the menu) followed by a number indicating the number of    *
 *   servings of that food. A sample input line would be:          *
 *                                                                 *
 *                    1 2    13 4    9 5    0 0                     *
 *   The sequence of serving description terminates with a         *
 *   description of item 0 (any number of servings will do).       *
 *        The output of the program is the calorie value of        *
 *   the meal.                                                      *
 *  ------------------------------------------------------------  *)
    const
       MAXFOOD    = 19;
       STRINGSIZE = 25;
    type
       FOODCODES = 1..MAXFOOD;
       STRING = packed array [1..STRINGSIZE] of CHAR;
    var
       FOODNAME: array [FOODCODES] of STRING;
       ENERGYVALUE: array [FOODCODES] of integer;
       ITEM: 0..MAXFOOD;
       NUMSERVINGS,CALORIES: integer;

begin
    (* Initialize variables *)
    FOODNAME[1]     := 'Milk, whole..1 cup         ';
    ENERGYVALUE[1]  := 159;
    FOODNAME[2]     := 'Banana, 1/2 small          ';
    ENERGYVALUE[2]  :=  50;
    FOODNAME[3]     := 'Cantaloupe, 1/4 (6'' dia)  ';
    ENERGYVALUE[3]  := 150;
    FOODNAME[4]     := 'Tomato juice  1/2 cup      '.
    ENERGYVALUE[4]  := 100;
    FOODNAME[5]     := 'Grapefruit  1/2 small      ';
    ENERGYVALUE[5]  := 100;
    FOODNAME[6]     := 'Orange juice  1/2 cup      ';
    ENERGYVALUE[6]  := 100;
    FOODNAME[7]     := 'Bread, baker''s, 1 slice   ';
    ENERGYVALUE[7]  :=  25;
```

Program 7-3. The DIET Advice Program.

Program 7-3. Continued.

```
FOODNAME[8]       := 'Biscuit or Roll(2 in dia)   ';
ENERGYVALUE[8]    := 35;
FOODNAME[9]       := 'Muffin  (2 in dia)          ';
ENERGYVALUE[9]    := 40;
FOODNAME[10]      := 'Dry cereal, 3/4 cup         ';
ENERGYVALUE[10]   := 20;
FOODNAME[11]      := 'Oatmeal  1/2 cup cooked     ';
ENERGYVALUE[11]   := 100;
FOODNAME[12]      := 'Butter or Margarine 1 tsp   ';
ENERGYVALUE[12]   :=  5;
FOODNAME[13]      := 'Light cream  2 Tbsp         ';
ENERGYVALUE[13]   := 30;
FOODNAME[14]      := 'Coffee; black               ';
ENERGYVALUE[14]   :=  0;
FOODNAME[15]      := 'Sugar, tsp                  ';
ENERGYVALUE[15]   :=  4;
FOODNAME[16]      := 'Cheese, cheddar, 1 oz.      ';
ENERGYVALUE[16]   := 30;
FOODNAME[17]      := 'Egg, cooked, 1 medium       ';
ENERGYVALUE[17]   := 50;
FOODNAME[18]      := 'Bacon, crisp, 1 slice       ';
ENERGYVALUE[18]   := 10;
FOODNAME[19]      := 'Sausage, link(1)            ';
ENERGYVALUE[19]   := 60;

(* Display Menu *)
WRITELN( 'Breakfast Menu:');
WRITELN( '============== ');
for ITEM := 1 to MAXFOOD do
   WRITELN( ITEM:2 ,'...', FOODNAME[ITEM]);
WRITELN;
WRITELN( 'Please input your meal specification');
CALORIES    := 0;
ITEM        := 1;
NUMSERVINGS := 0;

(* Input the specification *)
repeat
   CALORIES   := CALORIES
                  + (NUMSERVINGS * ENERGYVALUE[ITEM]);
   READ(ITEM,NUMSERVINGS);
until ITEM = 0;
WRITELN;
WRITELN( 'The energy value of this meal is',
         CALORIES:5, ' calories.');
end.
```

7.3 Expanding Your Horizons

While much of the data we need to work with in ordinary life can be represented by simple tables, it is often convenient, and sometimes necessary, to make use of two-dimensional tables, and other more complex tables. For example, consider the following table of bolt tightening specifications for engines on Toyota automobiles. (Entries are in ft/lbs of force.)

Engine	RockerShaft	CamBearings	RockerArm	OilPan
8RC	14.5	14.5	5	4
18RC	14.5	14.5	5	4
3KC	15	0	2.5	2.5
2TC	58	0	4	5
2OR	58	9.5	10	4

Because of the generality of the declarations of arrays in Pascal, no separate facilities are needed for such two- or higher-dimensional tables. This is because the type of the variable in an array declaration can itself be an array type. Now since any two-dimensional table can be thought of as the list of its rows, then the two-dimensional table can be realized as an array of arrays in Pascal.

For example, we might represent the table above as follows:

```
type
    ENGINE = (E8RC, E18RC, E3KC, E2TC, E20R);
    PART = (ROCKERSHAFT, CAMBEARINGS,
                         ROCKERARM, OILPAN);
    ROW = array [PART] of real;
    TABLE = array [ENGINE] of ROW;
var
    BOLTS: TABLE;
```

Then the expression

```
BOLTS[ E18RC ]
```

refers to the row corresponding to engine 18RC, and the expression

```
BOLTS[ E18RC ][CAMBEARINGS]
```

refers to the CAMBEARINGS (i.e., second) entry in the 18RC (i.e., second) row.

Note that this last expression names a simple real variable. Therefore, to achieve the entry corresponding to the table above, we would use the assignment statement:

```
BOLTS[E18RC][CAMBEARINGS] := 14.5
```

To simplify this notation (and to conform more closely to common mathematical usage), Pascal permits us to abbreviate

```
BOLTS[E18RC][CAMBEARINGS]
```

by using

```
BOLTS[E18RC, CAMBEARINGS]
```

In a similar vein, we may use abbreviated declarations of higher dimensional arrays. Our definition of TABLE above is equivalent to

```
TABLE = array[ENGINES] of array[PARTS] of real;
```

This may be abbreviated as:

```
TABLE = array[ENGINES,PARTS] of real;
```

Since two-dimensional array types (such as TABLE) are perfectly good Pascal types, we may consider arrays of such objects yielding three-dimensional tables, and so forth. For example, given the type declarations presented above, we can go on to declare

```
YEAR = 1970..1980;
ALLBOLTS = array[YEAR] of TABLE;
```

This is equivalent to

```
ALLBOLTS = array[YEAR] of array[ENGINES]
              of array[PARTS] of real;
```

which is in turn equivalent to

```
ALLBOLTS = array[YEAR, ENGINE, PARTS] of real;
```

Thus if BOLTBOOK declared to be of type ALLBOLTS, then

```
BOLTBOOK[1975]
```

refers to the two-dimensional table for year 1975,

```
BOLTBOOK[1975,E18RC]
```

refers to a row in that table, and

```
BOLTBOOK[1975,E18RC,CAMBEARINGS]
```

refers to a single value in that row.

Exercises

Exercise 7-1 Write a version of the program CHANGE of Chapter 2 which utilizes enumeration types and arrays as follows. It makes use of an enumeration type:

```
COINAGE
  = (PENNIES,NICKELS,DIMES,QUARTERS,HALFDOLLARS,DOLLARS)
```

The variables it uses are:

```
NEXTCOIN : COINAGE;
COINVALUES,NUMCOINS : array[COINAGE] of integer;
NUMCENTS,NUMDOLLARS,TOTALCHANGE : integer;
```

Use for loops to execute the repetitive actions.

Exercise 7-2 Write a program FREQUENCY which reads text from the file INPUT and prints out on the terminal the frequency of each letter which it encounters. You will want to make use of a subrange type

```
LETTER = A..Z
```

together with an array[LETTER] of integer.

Exercise 7-3 The cost of bouquets at a florist's shop depends both on the numbers of each kind of component flower together with their colors. Write a program FLORIST which inputs descriptions of bouquets in terms of the numbers and colors of each kind of component flower, and which outputs the cost of the bouquet. Make use of the enumeration types

```
BLOSSOMS    = (AMARYLLIS, AZALEA, MUM, DAFFODIL, DAISY,
               GLADIOLUS, IRIS, LILAC, LILY, PANSY,
               PEONY,  PETUNIA, ROSE, VIOLET);
COLORS      = (WHITE, PINK, RED, ORANGE, YELLOW, GREEN,
               BLUE, INDIGO, VIOLET)
```

together with the two-dimensional arrays

```
COSTS,NUMFLOWERS : array[BLOSSOMS,COLORS] of integer
```

much as in Exercise 7-1.

Exercise 7-4 Write a program MECHANIC suitable for use in Toyota repair shops. It will input descriptions of bolts (as in Section 7.3) and will output the foot-pounds of force to use when tightening the given bolt. To this extent, the program is similar to those of Exercises 7-1 and 7-3. Note that the array BOLTBOOK is three-dimensional. However, the actual values to be entered in BOLTBOOK should not appear in the program itself. Instead, the main body of the program should begin with an initialization section which reads in the values from a file VALUES. Of course, the file can only store the values in sequential order. So you must assume that the values in the file are organized by YEAR, ENGINE, and PART, say with YEAR corresponding to pages of a book, ENGINE corresponding to lines on a page, and PART corresponding to horizontal position on the line. You need to use for loops to read in the data.

Exercise 7-5 Let TABLE be an array[1..MAXINDEX] of integer (or real). We say that TABLE is *sorted* if for all I and J with $1 < I < J <$ MAXINDEX, we have

TABLE[I] < TABLE[J]

Consider the following algorithm for sorting an arbitrarily given instance of TABLE:

Sweep through TABLE from TABLE[1] to TABLE[MAXINDEX] doing the following: At the Ith step, determine the smallest item among TABLE[I], . . . ,TABLE[MAXINDEX], and swap it with TABLE[I].

Write a program SELECTSORT which reads in the values for TABLE from the file INPUT, which then uses the algorithm above to sort TABLE, and then prints out TABLE in order on the terminal.

Exercise 7-6 An alternate algorithm for sorting TABLE (see Exercise 7-5) is as follows:

Make MAXINDEX passes over TABLE doing the following: successively compare adjacent elements of TABLE. When an out-of-order pair is encountered, exchange them, and work back up the array, comparing and exchanging this "small" element with those "above" it until it is in its correct position. (If one imagines the array standing vertically, one can think of the "small" element "bubbling up" to its correct position.)

Write a program BUBBLESORT which reads the values of TABLE in from the file INPUT, which uses the foregoing algorithm to sort TABLE, and which then prints out TABLE in order on the terminal.

Exercise 7-7 A final alternate algorithm for sorting TABLE (see the two preceding Exercises) is to use the card-player's selection method:

Start with TABLE[2] and make MAXINDEX–1 passes over TABLE doing the following: the sorted sequence is gradually built up starting at TABLE[1] and extending up to TABLE[I-1] at step I. One then selects TABLE[I] from the unsorted portion of TABLE, and inserts it into the correct place in the sorted portion, moving elements already present down as necessary.

Write a program CARDSORT which reads in the values of TABLE from the file INPUT, uses this algorithm to sort TABLE, and which then prints TABLE out in order on the terminal.

Exercise 7-8 Given that

SQUARE = array[1..K, 1..K] of real

where K is an integer, and given that

M,N,P : SQUARE

we say that the array P is the *matrix product* of the arrays M and N (and we write P = M*N) provided that for all i and j with 1<i, j<K, we have

P[i,j] =

$$M[i,1]*N[1,j] + M[i,2]*N[2,j] + \ldots + M[i,K]*N[K,j]$$

Write a procedure which takes three var parameters M,N, and P of type SQUARE as above. After the procedure finishes running, the relation P = M*N should hold. (Thus the procedure calculates M*N and outputs the result through the var parameter P.)

Chapter Eight

Steering the Conversation: Procedures and Functions

As programs grow larger and more complicated, it is easy to flounder in the resulting complexity. The time-honored method for navigating the shoals of complexity (in any area) is to divide and conquer. This is achieved in Pascal by using two types of subprograms: procedures and functions. The topics treated in this chapter include:

- Using subprograms to manage complexity.
- Realizing subcomputations as functions.
- Realizing subprograms as procedures.
- Passing arguments to procedures and functions.

8.1   Navigating the Shoals of Complexity

When programs grow beyond one page in length, they become difficult to read and understand. Our small examples are already growing beyond this limit. Large scale programs can grow to thousands and thousands of lines! At such sizes, the prospect would seem to be total unintelligibility! If the programs are not humanly intelligible, there is little hope that they could be correct! Fortunately, humanity's age-old device for dealing with complexity is also applicable here: divide the problem into pieces that are small enough to be managed in and of themselves, and then, when the pieces are correctly built, assemble them into the whole.

Of course, if there are too many pieces to be assembled into a whole, we have not licked the problem. So the entire process may take several iterations. First, one splits the total problem into a manageable number of subproblems. If any of these subproblems are simple enough, they are solved immediately. But for those subproblems that still remain forbiddingly complex, we apply the technique to them. The subproblem is split into a manageable number of sub-subproblems. Those that can be solved are finished off, and the others are split up again and so forth until, at some final level, all sub-sub- . . . subproblems have been solved. Then the assembly process proceeds back up the tree of sub-sub- . . . subproblems, putting each little manageable number of sub- sub- problems together and so on, until the whole is assembled. In fact, if the original analysis and decomposition phase is carefully done, the reconstruction phase is straightforward and simple.

Even if there were no linguistic facilities in Pascal to aid in this decomposition/reconstitution process, it would be an excellent way to tackle large programming problems. But the technique is all that much more powerful because Pascal provides excellent facilities for aiding its execution. These facilities amount to the ability to define subprograms within Pascal programs. These subprograms then naturally correspond to the subproblems, which we generate as we analyze the parent problem.

Let us tackle the following problem with these techniques. Our problem is to aid navigators sailing the oceans. (It would also aid navigators flying anywhere short of the moon.) The input to the program will be the sailor's starting and terminating locations. The output of the program will be the appropriate course for the sailor to follow.

In order to successfully carry this problem through, let us first sketch the necessary navigational background.

The problem of simply describing a position on the high seas is itself a problem of some sophistication. In coastal waters it is almost always possible to locate oneself relative to some distinguished coastal object, for example, three kilometers northeast of Nantucket lighthouse. But on the high seas, it is impossible to refer to any coastal landmarks since they are all far out of visual range. Instead, it becomes necessary to introduce an abstract system of coordinates, the system of *latitude* and *longitude*. In many ways this system resembles the system of addresses used in most cities, in which to specify a given building, one must specify the street or avenue on which the building is located, together with a numerical address that specifies the location of the building along the avenue. Moreover, this address is often coordinated with the streets crossing the given avenue, so that the address of the building on the avenue will reveal the nearest cross street as in Figure 8-1.

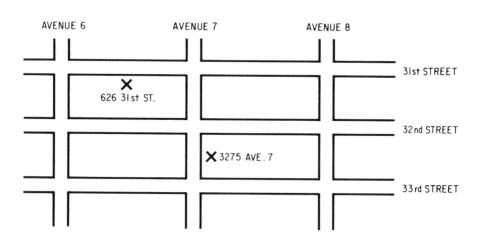

Figure 8-1.

The system of latitude and longitude provides a similar method of addressing any point on the surface of the earth. The avenues of our city example become the *meridians of longitude,* while the cross streets become the *parallels of latitude* as indicated in Figure 8-2.

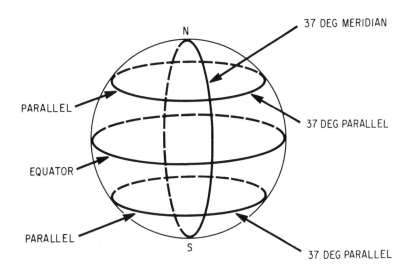

Figure 8-2.

As Figure 8-2 indicates, meridians of longitude are imaginary lines on the earth's surface that would result from slicing the globe with a knife (plane) through the north and south poles, while the parallels of latitude are lines that would result from slicing with a knife (plane) parallel to the equator.

To complete this system of addressing, we must assign a number or name to each meridian and parallel and show how this specifies the address. Here we introduce the notion of degree since we are in fact dealing with circles. Consequently, we could specify addresses along the equator by giving a degree: 37 degrees equator would specify a unique position along the equator, provided we knew the position specified by 0 degrees equator. At the present, most people agree to define 0 degrees equator to be the point on the equator that lies on the meridian of longitude passing through the naval observatory at Greenwich, England.

Having established the 0 degree position along the equator, we now divide the equator into 360 equal parts. The division points east of the 0 degree point are labeled with the positive integers 1,2,3, . . . ,180, while those west of the 0 degree point are labeled with the negative integers -1, -2, . . . -179. Points between are labeled with decimals so that we have such addresses as 34.66 and -78.93.

To provide the connections between our "avenues" and the "addresses" along the equator, we agree to name the meridians by the address on the equator through which they pass. Thus the meridian passing through 37 degrees equator is called the 37 degrees meridian. And to extend this connection to the parallels of latitude, we assign addresses along the parallels identical to the name of the intersecting meridian, as indicated in Figure 8-3.

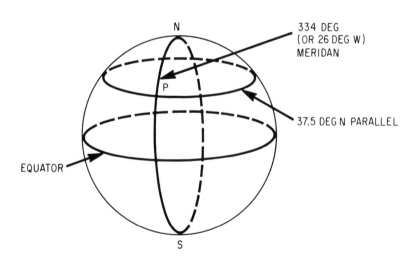

Figure 8-3.

To name the parallels of latitude, we proceed as follows. Consider the *prime meridian*, which is the meridian passing through the poles and Greenwich, England. We will assign degrees along this meridian just as we did along the equator. The zero point is taken to be the point where the prime meridian crosses the equator. Points north of the equator are given positive values +1, +2, . . . , +90, while points south are given negative values –1, –2, . . . , –90. The parallels of latitude are assigned names corresponding to the points where they cross the prime meridian. Finally, we assign addresses along all the meridians by giving them the name of the parallel passing through them, as Figure 8-3 indicates.

Consider the point P in Figure 8-3. Its location can be specified in each of the following ways:

1. 37.5 degrees on the –26 degree meridian.

2. –26 degrees on the 37.5 degree parallel.

3. The intersection of the 37.5 degree parallel with the –26 degree meridian.

The last way mentioned is the most common. It is what is meant when one speaks of P as being at latitude 37.5 and longitude –26.

Now that we have established a way of identifying every point on the globe, we can turn to the problem of navigating between two given points, A and B. Specifically, if we are at A and wish to get to B, in which direction should we sail?

The simplest method of sailing, using latitude and longitude, is the system called *plain* (or *plane*) *sailing*. This approach pretends that the earth is not a sphere but instead is a flat plane, so that the meridians are treated as parallel straight lines. Then all the machinery of simple trigonometry can be used in the computations. Thus, from the example of Figure 8-4, it is clear that we need to be able to calculate the angle X. Then we would simply point our ship X degrees north of the parallel (or 90 – X degrees east of the meridian).

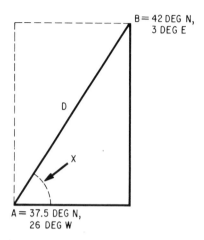

B = 42 DEG N,
3 DEG E

D

X

A = 37.5 DEG N,
26 DEG W

Figure 8-4.   The Navigation Problem.

In addition, we would also like to know how far it is from A to B.

Let us agree here to a convention that will simplify our calculations later. Namely, changes in latitude going due north or distance traveled going due north will be regarded as positive, while changes in latitude going due south and distances traveled going due south will be regarded as negative. Similarly, changes in longitude going due east or distances traveled going due east will be regarded as positive, while changes in longitude and distances traveled going due west will be regarded as negative.

We may now begin solving the Navigation Problem as follows. First compute the degrees of difference in latitude between A and B:

latitude difference(A,B) = 42 - 37.5 = 4.5 degrees
longitude difference(A,B) = 3 -(-26) = 2Ɔ degrees

Note that here we subtracted the coordinates of the point of departure from the coordinates of the destination. This rule holds fast for all navigational calculations.

Since the circumference of the earth is just about 40,000 kilometers and there are 360 degrees in a circle, each degree is approximately equal to 111.11 kilometers. Thus 4.5 degrees latitude change is equal to 500 km, while 29 degrees longitude change is equal to 3222 km. Consequently, our sailing diagram would appear as in Figure 8-5.

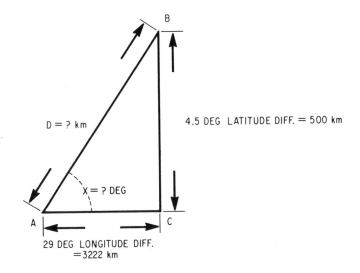

Figure 8-5.

If we know the lengths of the two legs of a right triangle, the methods used in the program ANGLE of Chapter 3 will enable us to find the angle we seek. And since in any right triangle

HYP = OPP * SIN(ANGLE)

we will be able to find the required distance from A to B using Pascal's built-in SIN function.

Thus we can now work out the entire problem. If the coordinates of the initial position are STARTLAT and STARTLONG, and if the coordinates of the finishing position are STOPLAT and STOPLONG, then letting

LATDIFF = STOPLAT – STARTLAT

and

LONGDIFF = STOPLONG – STARTLONG

the lengths of the legs of the triangle will be

NSLEG = 111.11 * LATDIFF

and

EWLEG = 111.11 * LONGDIFF

Consequently, if ANGLE is the desired course angle and DISTANCE is the required distance to be traveled, we have

ANGLE = arctan(NSLEG / EWLEG)

and

DISTANCE = NSLEG / sin(ANGLE)

In our example, ANGLE = 8.82 degrees and DISTANCE = 3260 km.

8.2   Packaged Conversations

We can now begin the process of building our program NAVIGATE. The essential actions are to input the required data (in this case the starting and finishing positions), compute the required quantities (here, the course angle and distance to be traveled), and output the results. Thus at the top level, our program can be outlined as in Figure 8-6.

```
program NAVIGATE;
(*  ------------------------------------------------------------  *
 *        This program computes a course between a starting       *
 *  and terminal position by plain sailing methods.               *
 *        The input to the program is the latitude and longitude  *
 *  of the starting and terminating positions.  These are all     *
 *  signed real numbers. For latitude, positive reals ranging     *
 *  from 0 to 90.0 denote northern latitudes, while reals ranging *
 *  from 0 to -90.0 denote southern latitudes. For longitude,     *
 *  positive reals ranging from 0 to 180.0 denote longitudes east *
 *  of the prime meridian, while negative reals ranging from 0    *
 *  to -180.0 denote longitudes west of the prime meridian.       *
 *        The output of the program consists of the plain sailing *
 *  course from starting to terminating point, together with      *
 *  the distance between these two points in kilometers.          *
 *  ------------------------------------------------------------  *)
begin
    Input the starting and finishing positions;

    Compute the course angle;

    Compute the course distance;

    Output the results;
end.
```

Figure 8-6. Outline of a Navigation Program.

Consider now the main computational portion of the program: the problem of computing the course angle and the course distance. Both of these computations are simple functions; they accept some inputs and return a computed value. Thus the function to compute the course angle must be given the latitudes and longitudes of the starting and finishing positions as input; it will return the course angle as its output. Likewise, the function to compute the course distance must be given the course angle together with, for example, the starting and stopping latitudes (from which it can compute the length of the north-south leg) as inputs; it returns the course distance as output.

Instead of requiring us to directly insert the code that computes these functions at the precise place where it is needed in the main program, Pascal allows us to bundle these bits of code into subprograms with names. Then at the exact point where the function is we simply "call" or "run" the subprogram, supplying it with the appropriate inputs. In addition, we are allowed to actually say what the code is and to compute these functions elsewhere in the program. This has a simple, useful property: for if we need to compute a given function at more than one place in the program, we need only write the code once at the place where we actually define the function. Then, at the places where we need to use this code, we can "call" the function by name, handing it the appropriate inputs. But more importantly, this provides us with a concrete linguistic tool to reflect the general problem-solving strategy of divide and conquer. The solution methods for each subproblem are bundled into linguistically separate functions. Even if a given function is "called" at only one place in the program, it is worth separating its actions from those of the other subproblem solutions.

So if all of this divide and conquer methodology is so great, how do we do it? There are two things we must learn: how to define a function and how to use it. The first step, as with almost everything else in programming, is to choose a name for the function. In the case of our course angle computation, let us use COMPCOURSE as the name for the function. Of course, we must tell Pascal about our choice. What are the things we must convey in addition to the simple name itself? They are:

- The nature of the inputs it requires.

- The nature of its output.

- The nature of its computation.

All three things are bundled into two parts of the function declaration: a *function header* and a *function body*. They are exactly like the corresponding *program header* and *program body* that make up all of our programs. For example, the declaration for COMPCOURSE takes the following form:

```
function COMPCOURSE(STARTLAT,STARTLONG,
                STOPLAT, STOPLONG : real) : real;
     Remainder of function header;
     Function body;
```

The reserved word *function* tells Pascal that a function is being defined (or declared). This is followed by the name of the function. Then following the function name comes information describing the inputs to the function. This information is enclosed in parentheses. The input information consists of a name for each variable (for use in the function body) together with an indication concerning the type each variable is to be. This type information is conveyed by following the variable with a colon and the name of the type. Thus it is like a variable declaration. And like our ordinary variable declarations, several input variables of the same type may be grouped together as we have done. In our example, we have said that all of the inputs will be of type real. Finally, the type of the output of the function is declared by following the parenthesized list of input information by a colon and the name of the type of the output. Again, in our example, the type is real. All of this information (that is, the declaration) is seperated from what follows by a semicolon.

This information is followed by declarations of constants, types, variables, and other functions and procedures that are strictly *local* to this function. These declarations are like ordinary declarations in form and meaning. Following these local declarations is the function body. This body is simply a Pascal statement in the form of a compound statement (begin . . . end), even if it only has one operational statement in it.

To start with a small example, consider defining a function CUBE which will take as input one integer and return the cube of that integer as output. It can be defined by the following declaration:

```
function CUBE(ARGIN : integer) : integer;
begin
   CUBE := ARGIN * ARGIN * ARGIN;
end
```

This example fits all of our prescriptions above except one: it appears that its sole operational statement is not an acceptable Pascal statement because the identifier CUBE hasn't been declared to be an integer variable, though it is used in the position of one. However, it is just this use that tells Pascal what the value of the function is to be at the end of the computation. Thus the function name can apparently be used as a variable of the type that the function expects to return. However, this use is restricted: the "variable" can only be assigned to; it cannot be read from. Therefore, we can only use the function name on the left side of assignment statements. Such statements simply state what value the function will return.

For a similarly simple function, consider the function that converts degrees to radians. That is, given the size of an angle measured in degrees, it returns the size measured in radians. You will recall that the relationship between radians and degrees is indicated by the proportion:

$$\frac{radians}{pi} = \frac{degrees}{180}$$

Thus given DEGREES, the corresponding RADIANS would be

```
RADIANS = (DEGREES * PI) / 180
```

The following function definition encapsulates all of this:

```
function DEGREESTORADIANS(DEGREES : real) : real;
begin
    DEGREESTORADIANS := (DEGREES * PI) / 180;
end
```

Of course, we presume the constant PI has been properly declared in any program in which we would use this definition.

The inverse function, which converts radian measures back to degrees, is defined by:

```
function RADIANSTODEGREES(RADIANS : real) : real;
begin
    RADIANSTODEGREES := (RADIANS * 180) / PI;
end
```

Now consider a slightly more complex example. This time we wish to define a function INTEGRALCUBEROOT that when given a non-negative real input (ARGIN), will return the largest integer whose cube is less than or equal to ARGIN. For negative inputs, the function will return 0. The following declaration will define this function:

```
function INTEGRALCUBEROOT( ARGIN : real ) : integer;
    var
        COUNTER : integer;
begin
    if ARGIN <= 0 then
        INTEGRALCUBEROOT := 0
    else
    begin
        COUNTER := 1;

        while (COUNTER * COUNTER * COUNTER) <= ARGIN do
            COUNTER := COUNTER + 1;

        INTEGRALCUBEROOT := COUNTER - 1;
    end;
end
```

This definition shows that the function identifier, in this case INTEGRALCUBEROOT, can occur at several different places in the body of the function. However, at each place, it is only assigned.

This declaration has another very interesting aspect: it contains a *local* variable declaration. In the section of the function header following the function statement, there is a *var* declaration, namely that the identifier COUNTER is declared to be an integer variable. This declaration is, of course, permitted by Pascal. (We wouldn't have made it otherwise.) Since this variable will be used by the function INTEGRAL-CUBEROOT alone, it is declared here instead of in the main program declaration section. This makes it private to INTEGRALCUBEROOT. Consequently, there is no way it can become entangled with a similarly named variable in some other section of the program. We will have more to say about this later.

With these observations about the use and declaration of functions in mind, we can revise our outline of NAVIGATE as shown in Figure 8-7.

```
program NAVIGATE;
(*  ------------------------------------------------------------  *
 *        This program computes a course between a starting       *
 *   and terminal position by plain sailing methods.              *
 *        The input to the program is the latitude and longitude  *
 *   of the starting and terminating positions.  These are all    *
 *   signed real numbers. For latitude, positive reals ranging    *
 *   from 0 to 90.0 denote northern latitudes, while reals ranging *
 *   from 0 to -90.0 denote southern latitudes. For longitude,    *
 *   positive reals ranging from 0 to 180.0 denote longitudes east *
 *   of the prime meridian, while negative reals ranging from 0   *
 *   to -180.0 denote longitudes west of the prime meridian.      *
 *        The output of the program consists of the plain sailing *
 *   course from starting to terminating point, together with     *
 *   the distance between these two points in kilometers.         *
 *  ------------------------------------------------------------  *)

    var
        STARTLAT, STARTLONG, STOPLAT,
        STOPLONG, COURSE,    DISTANCE  : real;

    function COMPCOURSE(STARTLAT,  STARTLONG,
                        STOPLAT,   STOPLONG  :real) : real;
        Rest of COMPCOURSE header;
        Body of COMPCOURSE;

    function DISTANCE(STARTLAT,STOPLAT,COURSE : real) : real;
        Rest of DISTANCE header;
        Body of DISTANCE;

begin

    Input the starting and finishing positions;

    COURSE :=
        COMPCOURSE(STARTLAT,STARTLONG,STOPLAT,STOPLONG);

    DISTANCE := COMPDISTANCE(STARTLAT,STOPLAT,COURSE);

    Output the results;

end.
```

Figure 8-7.   Using Functions in NAVIGATE.

Now let us build the functions COMPCOURSE and COMPDISTANCE. We will review the steps necessary to compute the course angle:

1. Compute the differences in latitude and longitude; let us use the variables LATDIFF and LONGDIFF for these quantities.

2. Compute the length of the north-south leg of the sailing triangle; let us use the variable NSLEG for this quantity.

3. Compute the length of the east-west leg of the sailing triangle; let us use EWLEG as the variable for this quantity.

4. Compute the quotient NSLEG/EWLEG and apply the ARCTAN function to this quantity to obtain the course angle.

None of the variables mentioned in this sequence have yet been defined in the main program. Since it appears that they will only be used by COMPCOURSE, we will declare them locally to COMPCOURSE.

One final note. The input positions are measured in degrees. However, Pascal's built-in trigonometric functions measure angles in radians. Thus we will need a function to convert from degrees to radians. Of course, this is the function DEGREESTORADIANS that we have just defined. Similarly, the output of Pascal's built-in ARCTAN function is in radians, but we would like to output the course angle in degrees. Consequently, we will also make use of the function RADIANS-TODEGREES, which we also defined earlier. We can now define COMPCOURSE as follows:

```
function COMPCOURSE(STARTLAT, STARTLONG,
                 STOPLAT, STOPLONG : real) : real;
    var
        LATDIFF, LONGDIFF,
        NSLEG, EWLEG,    RADIANCOURSE : real;
begin
    LATDIFF  := (STOPLAT - STARTLAT);
    LONGDIFF := (STOPLONG - STARTLONG);

    NSLEG    := LATDIFF * KMPERDEG;
    EWLEG    := LONGDIFF * KMPERDEG;

    RADIANCOURSE := ARCTAN( NSLEG / EWLEG );
    COMPCOURSE   := RADIANSTODEGREES( RADIANCOURSE );
end
```

To obtain the course distance, we must:

1. Compute the length of the north-south leg of the sailing triangle; let us use NSLEG for this variable.

2. Divide NSLEG by the result of applying the SIN function to the course angle.

Recalling that the course will be given by COMPCOURSE in degrees, we see that COMPDISTANCE may be defined as follows:

```
function COMPDISTANCE(STARTLAT,STOPLAT,
                      COURSE : real) : real;
   NSLEG : real;
begin
   NSLEG    := (STOPLAT - STARTLAT) * KMPERDEG;
   COMPDISTANCE :=
         NSLEG / SIN(DEGREESTORADIANS(COURSE));
end; (* COMPDISTANCE *)
```

Note that the function DEGREESTORADIANS is used in both the functions COMPCOURSE and COMPDISTANCE. We may now refine NAVIGATE as shown in Figure 8-8.

Figure 8-8. Adding Function Definitions to NAVIGATE.

```
program NAVIGATE;
(*  ------------------------------------------------------------  *
 *       This program computes a course between a starting        *
 *  and terminal position by plain sailing methods.               *
 *       The input to the program is the latitude and longitude   *
 *  of the starting and terminating positions.  These are all     *
 *  signed real numbers. For latitude, positive reals ranging     *
 *  from 0 to 90.0 denote northern latitudes, while reals ranging *
 *  from 0 to -90.0 denote southern latitudes. For longitude,     *
 *  positive reals ranging from 0 to 180.0 denote longitudes east *
 *  of the prime meridian, while negative reals ranging from 0    *
 *  to -180.0 denote longitudes west of the prime meridian.       *
 *       The output of the program consists of the plain sailing  *
 *  course from starting to terminating point, together with      *
 *  the distance between these two points in kilometers.          *
 *  ------------------------------------------------------------  *)
   const
      PI = 3.1416;
      KMPERDEG = 111.11;

   var
      STARTLAT, STARTLONG, STOPLAT,
      STOPLONG, COURSE,    DISTANCE    : real;
```

Figure 8-8. Continued.

```
function COMPDISTANCE(STARTLAT,STOPLAT,
                     COURSE : real) : real;
    var
       NSLEG : real;
    begin
       NSLEG   := (STOPLAT - STARTLAT) * KMPERDEG;

       COMPDISTANCE :=
             NSLEG / SIN(DEGREESTORADIANS(COURSE));
    end;  (* COMPDISTANCE *)

begin (* MAIN PROGRAM *)

    function DEGREESTORADIANS(DEGREES : real) : real;
       begin
          DEGREESTORADIANS := (DEGREES * PI) / 180
       end;  (* DEGREESTORADIANS *)

    function RADIANSTODEGREES(RADIANS : real) : real;
       begin
          RADIANSTODEGREES := (RADIANS * 180) / PI;
       end; (* RADIANSTODEGREES *)

    function COMPCOURSE(STARTLAT, STARTLONG,
                        STOPLAT,  STOPLONG : real) : real;
       var
          LATDIFF, LONGDIFF, MIDLAT,
          NSLEG,   EWLEG,    RADIANCOURSE : real;
       begin
          LATDIFF  := (STOPLAT - STARTLAT);
          LONGDIFF := (STOPLONG - STARTLONG);
          NSLEG    := LATDIFF * KMPERDEG;
          EWLEG    := LONGDIFF * KMPERDEG;

          RADIANCOURSE := ARCTAN(NSLEG / EWLEG);
          COMPCOURSE   := RADIANSTODEGREES(RADIANCOURSE);
       end;  (* COMPCOURSE *)
```

Input the starting and finishing positions;

```
COURSE   :=
     COMPCOURSE(STARTLAT,STARTLONG,STOPLAT,STOPLONG);
DISTANCE := COMPDISTANCE(STARTLAT,STOPLAT,COURSE);
```

Output the results;
```
end.
```

Our navigation program is nearly complete: we need only refine the input-output portions. The input portion presents no problem: we will treat it just as we have treated similar input in previous programs. The output, of course, is no real problem either. However, let us arrange to produce a traditional description of the output. That is, if we are to sail north with a course angle between 0 and 90 degrees, this would be described as north of east and so on. The table below presents these descriptions in their relation to the COURSE angle.

Sailing Direction	Course Angle	Description
North	Course > 0	North of east
North	Course < 0	North of west
South	Course < 0	South of east
South	Course > 0	South of west

We could, of course, just put a piece of code in the body of the main program to realize this table in the output message. However, let us encapsulate it into a separate routine. Note, though, that this routine does not compute any value. Instead, it causes something (a "side-effect") to occur: a message is printed on the terminal. Such routines are bundled up as *procedures* in Pascal.

The general form for procedures is similar to that for functions:

```
procedure identifier(parameter declarations);
    Rest of procedure header;
    Body of procedure;
```

Thus the fundamental difference between procedures and functions is simply that functions can return a value, while procedures cannot. Typically, we use procedures where we desire a side-effect to occur (such as some type of output), and we require that functions only compute values and not cause any side-effects. (We will discuss this point further in the next section.)

With this in mind, the following procedure would produce the desired output for our program:

```
procedure PRINTCOURSE(COURSE,STARTLAT,STOPLAT : real);
begin
   WRITELN;
   WRITE('The required course is ');

   if COURSE >= 0 then
      begin
         WRITE(COURSE:6:2);
         if STOPLAT >= STARTLAT then
            WRITELN(' degrees north of east.')
         else
            WRITELN(' degrees south of west.');
      end
   else
      begin
         WRITE(ABS(COURSE):6:2);
         if STOPLAT >= STARTLAT then
            WRITELN(' degrees north of west.')
         else
            WRITELN(' degrees south of east.')
      end;
end
```

With this definition in hand, we can now make the final refinement of NAVIGATE, producing the final program in Program 8-1.

Program 8-1. A Program for Navigational Advice.

```
program NAVIGATE;
(*  ------------------------------------------------------------  *
 *       This program computes a course between a starting        *
 *  and terminal position by plain sailing methods.               *
 *       The input to the program is the latitude and longitude   *
 *  of the starting and terminating positions.  These are all     *
 *  signed real numbers.  For latitude, positive reals ranging    *
 *  from 0 to 90.0 denote northern latitudes, while reals ranging *
 *  from 0 to -90.0 denote southern latitudes.  For longitude,    *
 *  positive reals ranging from 0 to 180.0 denote longitudes east *
 *  of the prime meridian, while negative reals ranging from 0    *
 *  to -180.0 denote longitudes west of the prime meridian.       *
 *       The output of the program consists of the plain sailing  *
 *  course from starting to terminating point, together with      *
 *  the distance between these two points in kilometers.          *
 *  ------------------------------------------------------------  *)
    const
       PI = 3.1416;
       KMPERDEG  = 111.11;

    var
       STARTLAT, STARTLONG, STOPLAT,
       STOPLONG, COURSE,    DISTANCE     : real;

    function DEGREESTORADIANS(DEGREES : real) : real;
       begin
          DEGREESTORADIANS := (DEGREES * PI) / 180;
       end;  (* DEGREESTORADIANS *)

    function RADIANSTODEGREES(RADIANS : real) : real;
       begin
          RADIANSTODEGREES := (RADIANS * 180) / PI;
       end; (* RADIANSTODEGREES *)
```

Program 8-1. Continued.

```
function COMPCOURSE(STARTLAT, STARTLONG,
                    STOPLAT, STOPLONG : real) : real;
   var
      LATDIFF, LONGDIFF,
      NSLEG, EWLEG,       RADIANCOURSE : real;
begin
   LATDIFF  := (STOPLAT - STARTLAT);
   LONGDIFF := (STOPLONG - STARTLONG);

   NSLEG    := LATDIFF * KMPERDEG;
   EWLEG    := LONGDIFF * KMPERDEG;

   RADIANCOURSE := ARCTAN(NSLEG / EWLEG);
   COMPCOURSE   := RADIANSTODEGREES(RADIANCOURSE);
end;  (* COMPCOURSE *)

function COMPDISTANCE(STARTLAT,STOPLAT,
                      COURSE : real) : real;

   var
      NSLEG : real;

   begin
     NSLEG  := (STOPLAT - STARTLAT) * KMPERDEG;

     COMPDISTANCE :=
          NSLEG / SIN(DEGREESTORADIANS(COURSE));
   end;  (* COMPDISTANCE *)


procedure PRINTCOURSE(COURSE,STARTLAT,STOPLAT : real);
   begin
      WRITELN;
      WRITE('The required course is ');

     if COURSE >= 0 then
         begin
            WRITE(COURSE:6:2);
            if STOPLAT >= STARTLAT then
              WRITELN(' degrees north of east.')
            else
              WRITELN(' degrees south of west.');
         end
      else
         begin
            WRITE(ABS(COURSE):6:2);
            if STOPLAT >= STARTLAT then
              WRITELN(' degrees north of west.')
            else
              WRITELN(' degrees south of east.')
         end;
   end; (* PRINTCOURSE *)
```

Program 8-1. Continued.

```
begin (* MAIN PROGRAM *)

    WRITE( 'Input your starting position: ');
    READ( STARTLAT, STARTLONG);
    WRITE( 'Input your terminal position: ');
    READ( STOPLAT, STOPLONG);

    COURSE :=
        COMPCOURSE(STARTLAT,STARTLONG,STOPLAT,STOPLONG);
        DISTANCE := COMPDISTANCE(STARTLAT,STOPLAT,COURSE);

        PRINTCOURSE(COURSE,STARTLAT,STOPLAT);
        WRITELN('The distance to be traveled is ',
            DISTANCE:8:2, ' KM.');
end.
```

Functions and procedures have turned out to be versatile and powerful devices for managing the complexity of more ambitious programs. Virtually any bit of Pascal code can be bundled up inside either one, and internally, they behave as if they were virtually independent programs.

However, like all good powerful tools, their incorrect use can lead to harm, if not disaster. Obviously, if almost every little piece of code is bundled willy-nilly into either a function or procedure with no regard for natural intuitive grouping, almost total disaster will result. The program (by chance) just might run, but it will in all likelihood be totally incomprehensible to a human reader. Our goal is to write correct Pascal programs that are lucid (nay, even compelling!) for the human reader. Consequently, one should take care that the use of procedures and functions reflects the natural breakdown of the overall problem into its components. Thus in NAVIGATE, computing the course (COMPCOURSE), computing the distance to be traveled (COMP-DISTANCE), and outputting the course in traditional format (PRINT-COURSE) are all natural components of the problem of providing navigational advice. Moreover, converting degrees to radians (DEGREES-TORADIANS) and radians to degrees (RADIANSTODEGREES) constitute natural subcomponents of these basic components.

Therefore, your overall strategy should be to analyze your problem naturally and intuitively (as a human) into manageable subproblems, then devise procedures and functions corresponding to these naturally occurring subproblems. Tackle each subproblem in the same way. When subproblems have common sub-subproblems, these common parts can be brought out into one common procedure or function independent of the subproblems, as we did in NAVIGATE with DEGREESTORADIANS and RADIANSTODEGREES.

The ability to produce understandable programs is increased by maintaining a discipline about the uses to which functions versus procedures are put. Specifically, only use functions to compute the value they return, and never allow them to produce any side-effects. Instead, only allow side-effects to be produced from procedures (or from the body of the main program). This is an extension of the divide and conquer philosophy. By separating these uses, one further manages the complexity. Consequently, a reader of a program in which such a discipline is maintained can expect, when reading a function definition, to concentrate on the computation of a value and not have to worry about other matters.

8.3   Telling Them What They Need To Know

The notion of local entities was touched briefly in the last section. Here we must consider it more extensively. Any entity that is declared inside a function or procedure declaration is said to be *local* to that function or procedure. Thus the identifier NSLEG is declared local to the function COMPDISTANCE in the program NAVIGATE. In this case, NSLEG is declared to be a real variable in COMPDISTANCE. You will recall that such a declaration assocites a real number "container" with the identifier NSLEG. Since this declaration is local to COMP-DISTANCE, only entities living inside of COMPDISTANCE (as well as COMPDISTANCE itself) can see this particular association between NSLEG and that real number container. In this sense, the association is private to COMPDISTANCE.

But what about COMPCOURSE! It too has a local declaration of NSLEG to be a real variable! Does it get left out? Of course not. The story of these two functions and their declarations of NSLEG is that each of them gets to have its own private association of NSLEG with a real number container, but the containers for each are different. Neither can see the other's association, as Figure 8-9 suggests.

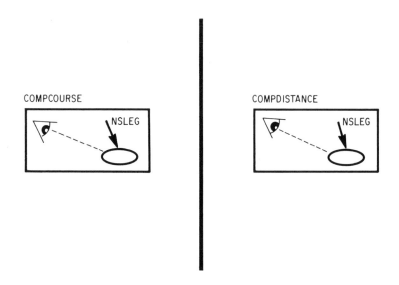

Figure 8-9.   Two Views of NSLEG.

How this comes about is none of our concern. We only need know that this is how the Pascal system deals with local declarations. In fact, it treats all local declarations in this way, whether they are variable, constant, type, function, or procedure declarations. The effect of a declaration is to associate some of Pascal entity with an identifier. If the declaration is local to a given function or procedure, only the beings inside that function can see that association.

Thus if there are types or functions or procedures that are needed only by some one function, such as MYFUNCTION, then those types or functions or procedures should be declared local to MYFUNCTION. Such actions have two positive benefits:

■ They further clarify the logical structure of the program for the human reader, since keeping things declared locally shows where they are used.

■ They prevent inadvertent clashes of declarations between different parts of the program. For example, suppose J is declared to be an integer variable in the main program, and is genuinely used in some portions of the main program body. Suppose also that a subsidiary function, MYFUNCTION, uses J for an index in a for-statement and that J is not declared locally in MYFUNCTION. If in fact J is really used in the main program and used in the same region MYFUNCTION is called and runs, the effect of this run of MYFUNCTION may be to change the value of J in a way that is total anathema to the main program! If J is declared locally to MYFUNCTION, this clash will be avoided because MYFUNCTION will get its own private association of J with an integer container that is distinct from the container associated with J in the main program.

The opposite of local is *global*. An entity (be it constant, type, variable, function, or procedure) is global to a given function or procedure, such as MYROUTINE, if it is either declared in the main program declarations or is declared in some function or procedure that contains the declaration of MYROUTINE. This can even extend to repeated nesting of declarations. Thus, suppose the following baroque situation: KENSROUTINE is declared in LYDIASROUTINE which in turn is declared in MELLISSASROUTINE. Then any entity that is also declared in MELISSASROUTINE is global to KENSROUTINE. So, for example, if WEEK is declared to be an enumeration type (as we did earlier) in MELISSASROUTINE, and if DAY is clared to be of type WEEK and this declaration is also in MELISSASROUTINE, then both WEEK and DAY are global to both KENSROUTINE and to LYDIASROUTINE.

When a declaration is global to a given function or procedure, that declaration can be seen by the given function or procedure. Thus both KENSROUTINE and LYDIASROUTINE can see the declarations of WEEK and DAY and can use and refer to them. Thus in KENSROUTINE we may declare YESTERDAY to be of type WEEK without having to worry about the declaration of WEEK: it has already been taken care of.

On the other hand, suppose ALEXSROUTINE is also declared inside LYDIASROUTINE but outside of KENSROUTINE. Then things declared inside KENSROUTINE cannot be seen by ALEXSROUTINE. In particular, the declaration of YESTERDAY made inside of KENSROUTINE could not be used or referred to inside of ALEXSROUTINE (nor for that matter in the bodies of LYDIASROUTINE and MELISSASROUTINE, nor in the main body of the program). Figure 8-10 illustrates the situation.

MELISSASROUTINE

```
                        WEEK = (...
                        DAY : WEEK

    LYDIASROUTINE
                        ALEXSROUTINE



    KENSROUTINE
                YESTERDAY : WEEK
```

Figure 8-10. The World According to . . .

The identifiers used to name the variables that are the inputs to a function or procedure are called the *formal parameters* of the function or procedure. (This is a bit of jargon, but we do need some sort of name, and that's what's used in the computer world.) Thus those identifiers occurring on the left sides of colons between the parentheses following the function or procedure name are the formal parameters. For example, the formal parameters of COMPCOURSE are

STARTLAT STARTLONG STOPLAT STOPLONG

The formal parameters of COMPDISTANCE are

STARTLAT STOPLAT COURSE

The formal parameters of a function or procedure, being identifiers, are declared by their occurrences in the function or procedure line. As we noted earlier, the forms of their occurrences were in shape just like declarations. Now we can say that they really are declarations. The most important point to note now is this: these declarations of the formal parameters are normally local to the function or procedure just like any declarations in the var section of the function or procedure heading. Thus the associations between the identifiers that are the formal parameters and the various "containers" are private to the function or procedure and cannot be seen by entities living outside the function or procedure.

When the function or procedure is called or used in some surrounding procedure or function or in the main body of the program, the effect is this: the expression occupying the position corresponding to a formal parameter in the call is evaluated, and this value is copied over into the variable or container associated with the formal parameter. This is done for all the formal parameters. Then the body of the function or procedure begins execution. This means of telling the function or procedure what it needs to know from the outside world is termed *call by value* (see Figure 8-11).

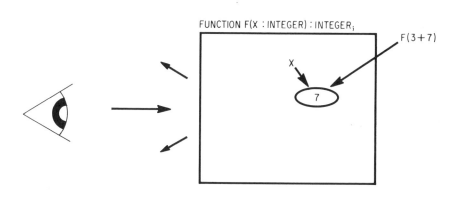

Figure 8-11. Call by Value.

Now any kind of object can be grist for input to a function or procedure. Not only simple scalar objects, such as integers or elements of enumeration types, but also arrays, files, records (when we learn about them), and (would you believe it!) even functions and procedures. Unfortunately, functions are not so generous with their output. Only scalars are permitted as the output of functions. In the program DIET

(Chapter 7), for example, we might define a little procedure to take care of writing out a line of the menu:

```
procedure MENULINE(NUM : integer; DESCRIP : STRING);
    WRITELN(NUM:2, '...', DESCRIP);
end
```

Here STRING is the type packed array[1..STRINGSIZE] of char, and so the object that MENULINE would expect to get for DESCRIP would be such an array. If we included this declaration of MENULINE in the program DIET, we could then rewrite the for statement that outputs the menu as

```
for ITEM := 1 to MAXFOOD do
    MENULINE(ITEM,FOODNAME[ITEM])
```

Now suppose that rather than bundling the writing of one line, we wish to bundle up the writing out of the menu. What we would like to do is the following:

```
procedure PRINTMENU(NAMELIST :
                         array[1..STRINGSIZE] of STRING);
var
      ITEM : 1..MAXFOOD;
begin
    WRITELN( 'Breakfast Menu:');
    WRITELN( '================');
    for ITEM := 1 to MAXFOOD do
        WRITELN(ITEM:2, '...', NAMELIST[ITEM]);
end
```

Conceptually, what we have said is meaningful to Pascal. However, it will not accept the precise way we have written it. Pascal requires that in the declarations of formal parameters in procedure and function headings, the quantities on the right sides of the colons be simple identifiers naming types. Simpleminded as it is, Pascal can't cope with complex type descriptions in these positions. So what we need is to have given the type

```
array[1..STRINGSIZE] of STRING
```

a simple name in a type declaration in the main program. Thus if we include the type declaration

```
DESCRIPTIONLIST = array[1..STRINGSIZE] of STRING
```

then we may change the declaration of FOODNAME to

```
FOODNAME : DESCRIPTIONLIST
```

and we may define PRINTMENU by:

```
procedure PRINTMENU(NAMELIST : DESCRIPTIONLIST);
    var
        ITEM : 1..MAXFOOD;
    begin
        WRITELN( 'Breakfast Menu:');
        WRITELN( '===============');
        for ITEM := 1 to MAXFOOD do
            WRITELN(ITEM:2, '...', NAMELIST[ITEM]);
    end
```

Then at the appropriate point in the body of DIET, we would issue the call

```
PRINTMENU( FOODNAME )
```

The effect of the call is this: the entire contents of the array variable FOODNAME are copied over into the corresponding portions of the private variable or container associated with NAMELIST for PRINTMENU, and then the body of PRINTMENU begins executing. The overall effect is exactly what we had before.

Call by value, which we have discussed, has the same advantage that other local declarations have: the variables associated with the formal parameters cannot get tangled up with any other variables in the program. In particular, if the actual values passed into the procedure or function are simply contained in some global variables, nothing we do inside the procedure or function can affect those global variables. For example, suppose MYPROCEDURE has been defined by

```
procedure MYPROCEDURE(MYVAR : integer);
    begin
        . . .
        MYVAR := MYVAR + 9;
        . . .
    end
```

Moreover, suppose ANOTHERVAR has been declared to be an integer variable in the main program and that the following occurs in the body of the program:

```
    . . .
    ANOTHERVAR := 23;
    MYPROCEDURE(ANOTHERVAR);
    . . .
```

Then, among many other things, the following will happen:

1. ANOTHERVAR gets the value 23 assigned to its container.

2. When MYPROCEDURE is called, the value 23 is copied over into the container associated with MYVAR.

3. Sometime later, the indicated assignment statement in the body of MYPROCEDURE causes the value in the container associated with MYVAR to become 32.

4. When MYPROCEDURE finishes executing, MYVAR becomes unknown to the rest of the program (it is "wiped out").

However, note that since the containers associated with MYVAR and ANOTHERVAR are different, the value in the container associated with ANOTHERVAR is undisturbed by the action inside MYPROCEDURE. Hence when MYPROCEDURE finishes running, ANOTHERVAR still contains 23. In many cases it is important, of course, to keep a hold on a particular value, such as 23 in our sketch, even though that quantity must be passed to various routines for use. If Pascal did not provide the call by value mechanism, this would be a very tricky and difficult feat to accomplish.

Important as call by value is, it has a price: we must expend the effort of copying the input values into the variables associated with the formal parameters. This effort is considerable in the case of entities such as arrays (for example, in the case of FOODNAME in the program DIET). When necessary, of course, it must be done. But there are many circumstances when the procedure or function that will use the array is very careful not to try to assign to the formal parameters or in any other way tinker with them. In such a case, the copying effort necessary to carry out call by value seems to be a waste.

Pascal provides a mechanism that recognizes and deals with this problem. This mechanism is the *variable parameter* for functions and procedures. In essence, it allows us to inform Pascal that a given parameter of a function or procedure is not to be treated with the call by value mechanism. Instead, we guarantee that whenever the function or procedure is called, we will provide a *variable* as the actual input corresponding to the indicated parameter (as opposed to a complex expression that is permissible if the parameter is to be treated with call by value). In this case, Pascal does no recopying of the input value: it just uses the variable it was given directly. It is as if the actual variable used in the function call had been substituted for the formal parameter throughout the body of the function or procedure.

Obviously, this is a very valuable mechanism when passing arrays and other complex inputs to procedures and functions. One indicates that a parameter is to be treated as a variable parameter instead of a call by value parameter by preceding the parameter name with the reserved word *var* in the function or procedure line (that is, preceding the declaration of the identifier inside the parentheses following the procedure or function name in the declaration). Thus to make the parameter in PRINTMENU into a variable parameter, we would change the declaration to read

```
procedure PRINTMENU(var NAMELIST : DESCRIPTIONLIST);
   var
      ITEM : 1..MAXFOOD;
begin
   WRITELN( 'Breakfast Menu:');
   WRITELN( '================');
   for ITEM := 1 to MAXFOOD do
      WRITELN(ITEM:2, '...', NAMELIST[ITEM]);
end
```

The mechanism of the variable parameter also allows us to overcome one of the obvious shortcomings of Pascal's notion of function, namely, the fact that functions can only return scalars as values. If we wanted a function that returned, for example, a STRING (in the program DIET) as a value, we are out of luck since the type STRING is declared as an array. Fortunately, nothing in the notion of the variable parameter precludes us from putting the formal variable parameter on the left side of an assignment statement in the body of the procedure. Consequently, we may use this mechanism to pull a complex value back out of a procedure. We will discuss this topic in more detail in the next chapter in connection with the program MAKECABINET.

Exercises

Exercise 8-1   In 1730, James Stirling discovered the following approximation for the factorial of N:

SQRT(2*pi*N) * (N/e)**N

where pi and e are the famous constants with approximate values pi = 3.141159 and e = 2.71828. (Stirling's approximation gets better and better as N gets larger.) Write a Pascal function STIRLING which computes this approximation given argument N.

Exercise 8-2   Write Pascal functions which compute the following standard mathematical functions:

    i)   arcsin(x) = arctan(x/sqrt(1 - x*x)), x>0.
    ii)   arccos(x) = arctan((sqrt(1 - x*x)/x), x>0.
    iii)   sinh(x) = (exp(x) - exp(-x))/2.
    iv)   cosh(x) = (exp(x) + exp(-x))/2.
    v)   tanh(x) = sinh(x)/cosh(x).
    vi)   arcsinh(x) = ln(x + sqrt(x*x + 1)).
    vii) arccosh(x) = ln(x + sqrt(x*x - 1)).

Exercise 8-3   An amount P of money invested at interest rate R for N years compounded annually will have value

V = P*(1 + R)**N

at the end of that time. Write a Pascal function which takes P, R, and N as arguments, and returns V as its result.

Exercise 8-4   Dual to the notion of compounded principal (see Exercise 8-3) is the notion of present value. The *present value of a sum V at interest rate R over N years* is defined to be the principal P which if invested at rate R and compounded for N years would equal V. This is given by the formula:

P = V/(1 + R)**N

Write a Pascal function which takes V, R and N as arguments and returns P as its result.

Exercise 8-5 An *annuity* is a fixed sum A paid yearly over N years commencing some K years hence. The *present value* of such an annuity *at rate R* is the principal PV which, when invested today at rate R and compounded, would provide the same set of payments. This is given by:

PV = A[1/(1+R)**(K+1) + 1/(1+R)**(K+2) + . . . + 1/(1+R)**(K+N)].

Write a Pascal function which takes A, N, K, and R as arguments and returns PV as its result.

Exercise 8-6 Generation of statistically random sequences of integers is an important technique in computer programming. It has applications ranging from simulation of social and physical events to the programming of games. A sequence

> N0, N1, N2, . . . , Nk, . . .

which is statistically random can be defined as follows:

> Nk+1 = (MULTIPLIER * Nk + INCREMENT) mod MODULUS

where several choices for the constants will do:

> MODULUS = 65536 (= 2**16)
> INCREMENT = 13933
> MULTIPLIER = 1001

or

> MODULUS = 1024 (= 2**10)
> INCREMENT = 333
> MULTIPLIER = 1001

The first choice will produce a sequence of length 65,536 before it starts repeating, while the second will be only of length 1,024 before repetition occurs. Note that the initial value N0 is totally arbitrary (it is often called the *seed* for the sequence) and that the k+1st element Nk+1 of the sequence is defined in terms of the kth element Nk. Write a Pascal function RANDOM with no arguments which returns the successive elements of a random sequence each time it is called. That is, the first time RANDOM is called, it will return N0, the next time N1, and so forth. Make use of the equation given above together with a global variable SEED to store the initial value N0 and then the successive elements N1, N2, and so on.

Note: The initial value for SEED must be assigned some way. One method to utilize RANDOM would be to just assign some fixed value. The drawback is that the random sequence will be exactly the same each time the program is run. Another method would be to use another procedure RANDOMIZE to assign a value to SEED. If your Pascal system allows you to read such things as a system clock, RANDOMIZE could obtain the present date-time and use it for SEED. Or it could simply ask the user for an integer.

Exercise 8-7   Write a program COINTOSS which simulates the process of tossing a coin for runs of 10 tosses. The program should make use of the function RANDOM of Exercise 8-6. It should assign a value to SEED in some reasonable way to obtain random behavior. The input to the program should be the number of runs (of 10 tosses) to carry out. The output of the program should be a simple bar graph representing the frequencies obtained, for example:

```
Num Heads
0    *
1    ***
2    **
3    ****
4    ***********
5    **********************
6    *********************
7    **************
8    ******
9    ***
10   *
     _____
     0 1 2 3 4 5 6 7 8 9 . . .
```

Given an element Nk of the random sequence, test whether it is odd or even to simulate getting heads or tails on the coin. You should use an array[0 . . 10] of integer to store the frequencies during the generation of the runs. The printing of the bar graph should be encapsulated in a separate procedure which runs after the generation process is finished.

Exercise 8-8   If N0,N1, . . . ,Nk, . . . is a random sequence of integers, then calculating Nk mod C amounts to randomly choosing one of the integers 0,1,2, . . . ,C-1. Use this observation to construct a program DEALER which deals out bridge hands. That is, it divides a card deck into four groups of 13 cards each by a random method. One such method would amount to this: make use of enumeration types:

```
SUITS = (SPADES,HEARTS,DIAMONDS,CLUBS);
CARDS = (ACE,DEUCE,TREY,FOUR,FIVE,SIX,SEVEN,EIGHT,NINE,TEN,
         JACK,QUEEN,KING)
```

Then dealing a card could be simulated by randomly choosing a number from 0 to 3 to indicate the suit, and then randomly choosing a number from 0 to 12 to indicate the face value of the card. Of course, to simulate dealing from an actual deck, you must devise some method of keeping track of what cards have already been dealt, since a given card occurs only once in a deck. One method would be to use an array[SUITS,CARDS] of BOOLEAN. The value stored in each entry could indicate whether or not that card had been dealt.

Your program should contain at least two procedures, one DEAL which does the actual dealing. One method of storing the results of the deal would be to use four arrays NORTH, SOUTH, EAST, and WEST. These could be of type array[1 . . 13] of [0 . . 52]. The cards could be assigned numbers from 1 to 52 (use Pascal functions to do the coding and decoding!). The second procedure should print some reasonable representation of these hands on the terminal.

Note: After studying records in Chapter 9 we will have a much nicer method of representing cards and hands at our disposal.

Chapter Nine

Talented Talk: Records

It is a well-regarded talent to be able to talk easily about many topics in the world. Pascal's ability to do this is founded on its concept of record. The topics in this chapter will include:

- The concept of record.
- Using records to represent real-world entities.
- The contrasts between records and other composite types.
- Maintaining and manipulating files of records.

9.1   Picturing the World

A good description is one that captures the essential features of what it is describing. Which features are essential depend, of course, on the particular conversation. Human beings (a very common subject of conversation) can be described physically, or in terms of their earnings and expenses (the IRS talks about that!) or in terms of their criminal records (if any!), and so forth. For example, the Department of Motor Vehicles might describe Blaise Pascal in the following way on his driver's license:

Name: Pascal, Blaise
Street: 43 Rue Beaubourg
City: Paris
Date of Birth: 19 June 1643
Height: 157 cm
Weight: 63 kg
Eye Color: Brown
Corrective Lenses: Yes
Motorist Id : 2509664
License Expiration Date: 30 June 1648

Such a description usually includes a variety of data about the person or object. In our example there is numeric data (height, weight), literal data (name, street, and the like) and Boolean data (corrective lenses). It is all packaged together in one compact description.

lating such descriptions. These descriptions are called *records*. They can be thought of as a package of heterogeneous variables tied together. As such, one can declare a type for each kind of record one wishes to deal with. Thus, we might declare a type LICENSE as follows:

```
LICENSE = record
          NAME    : STRING;
          STREET  : STRING;
          CITY    : STRING;
          BIRTH   : DATE;
          HEIGHT  : integer;
          WEIGHT  : integer;
          EYES    : COLOR;
          LENSES  : BOOLEAN;
          IDNUM   : integer;
          EXPDATE : DATE;
        end;
```

In making this definition, we of course presume that we have previously defined the types STRING, DATE, and COLOR. As this example shows, the essence of the record declaration is a list consisting of the field names together with the types of objects intended for those fields. The elements of the list are in the form of variable declarations, separated as usual by commas. The entire list is delimited by the reserved words *record* and *end*.

Since the field specifications in the record definition are just like ordinary variable declarations, we can group those with the same type together, as with the ordinary declarations. Thus we could present the definition of LICENSE in the following form:

```
LICENSE = record
          NAME, STREET, CITY    : STRING;
          BIRTH, EXPDATE        : DATE;
          HEIGHT, WEIGHT, IDNUM : integer;
          EYES                  : COLOR;
          LENSES                : BOOLEAN
        end;
```

Once we have defined such a type, we may declare variables ranging over the objects of that type, as for example:

```
DRIVER : LICENSE;
```

The best way to think of this variable DRIVER is as a collection of individual variables, all bundled together. The individual variables range over the fields of the record. These individual variables are named by suffixing the record variable name with a dot followed by the field name. For example:

```
DRIVER.NAME,   DRIVER.BIRTH,  and  DRIVER.LENSES
```

Though the names for these variables are complex, they can be used exactly as any other variable of the same type. Thus we may assign values to them:

```
DRIVER.NAME   := 'Pascal, Blaise
DRIVER.LENSES := TRUE;
DRIVER.IDNUM  := 2509664
```

We may also read values from them. Thus

```
if DRIVER.LENSES then . . .
```

would be perfectly acceptable, as would

```
WRITE(DRIVER.CITY)
```

The fields of the record may themselves be records or arrays. In fact, the type STRING really is an array, as we noted earlier. We might in fact have made the following type definitions:

```
MONTH = (JAN, FEB, MARCH, APRIL, MAY, JUNE,
                JULY, AUGUST, SEPT, OCT, NOV, DEC);
DATE  = record
            DAY : 1..31;
            MON : MONTH;
            YEAR: integer
        end;
```

Then we may refer to the DRIVER's month of birth by

```
DRIVER.BIRTH.MON
```

and the year of the DRIVER's birth by

```
DRIVER.BIRTH.YEAR
```

In particular, if we are assigning to DRIVER the values for Blaise Pascal's license, we would write:

```
DRIVER.BIRTH.DAY  := 19;
DRIVER.BIRTH.MON  := JUNE;
DRIVER.BIRTH.YEAR := 1643
```

Consider another example. Imagine a talent agent maintaining records on her various clients. Besides name and address, the agent will need information on the person's sex, favored mediums for work, and skills. To build a record to represent such people, we could use a definition of

```
STRING = packed array [1..STRINGSIZE] of CHAR;
```

together with the following enumeration types:

```
GIGS   = (STAGE,SCREEN,NIGHTCLUB,VAUDEVILLE,
            TV,   RADIO, PLATTER,  POLITICS );
SKILLS = (DRAMA,COMEDY,VOCALIST, DANCER,
            INSTRUMENTALIST,      CAMPAIGNER);
SEXES  = (MALE,FEMALE);
```

Then we will define the agent's FOLDERs (which will later be put in the agent's file CABINET) by:

```
FOLDER = record
          NAME,ADDRESS,CITY : STRING;
          MEDIUM : GIGS;
          SEX    : SEXES;
          TALENT : SKILLS;
        end;
```

Now we can construct a FOLDER for Jacqueline Pascal, the young actress sister of Blaise Pascal. First, we must declare a variable of type FOLDER:

```
NEXTPERSON : FOLDER;
```

Then we assign values to the fields of this record variable by:

```
NEXTPERSON.NAME    := 'Pascal, Jacqueline  '.
NEXTPERSON.ADDRESS := '43 Rue Beaubourg    ';
NEXTPERSON.CITY    := 'Pars, France        ';
NEXTPERSON.MEDIUM  := STAGE;                 ;
NEXTPERSON.SEX     := FEMALE;
NEXTPERSON.TALENT  := DRAMA;
```

9.2   Filing the Pictures

Now let us construct a program TALENT which will enable our agent to rummage about through her file CABINET to retrieve the FOLDERs for people with specified SKILLS, SEX, and GIGS. As we did in Chapter 7, we will first assume that we may input and output enumeration types with the procedures READ and WRITE. With this assumption, the top-level design of our program appears in Figure 9-1.

```
program TALENT(INPUT, CABINET);
(*  ------------------------------------------------------------  *
 *        This program allows the user to search through the      *
 *   file CABINET looking for persons with various characteristics. *
 *   The entries in the file CABINET are FOLDERs, which are       *
 *   records. The fields of FOLDER are as follows: NAME,ADDRESS,  *
 *   CITYSTA,MEDIUM,SEX,TALENT.                                   *
 *        The input to this program consists of values for the   *
 *   MEDIUM, SEX, and TALENT fields.                             *
 *        The output of the program is the name and address for  *
 *   all FOLDERs that match the input field values.              *
 *  ------------------------------------------------------------  *)
      const
         STRINGSIZE = 20;
      type
         STRING = packed array [1..STRINGSIZE] of CHAR;
         GIGS = (STAGE,SCREEN,NIGHTCLUB,VAUDEVILLE,
                 TV,RADIO,RECORDING,POLITCS);
         SKILLS = (DRAMA,COMEDY,VOCALIST, DANCER,
                   INSTRUMENTALIST,       CAMPAIGNER);
         SEXES  = (MALE,FEMALE);
         FOLDER = record
                     NAME,ADDRESS,CITYSTA   : STRING;
                     MEDIUM  : GIGS;
                     SEX     : SEXES;
                     TALENT  : SKILLS;
                  end;
      var
         CABINET   : file of FOLDER;

begin

    Input values for MEDIUM, SEX, and TALENT;

    Work through CABINET comparing the input values for MEDIUM,

    SEX, and TALENT with those of each FOLDER, outputting the
        full record for each FOLDER for which they all match;

end.
```

Figure 9-1. A Program for Retrieving FOLDERs.

Our assumption that we may input enumeration types with READ makes the input portion of this quite easy. Let us use MEDIUMVAL, SEXVAL, and TALENTVAL as the variables for the inputs. For the remainder, we must first open the file CABINET with the statement:

```
reset(CABINET)
```

Then, as long as the file CABINET has more FOLDERs, we must get the next FOLDER and compare its values for the MEDIUM, SEX, and TALENT fields with those of MEDIUMVAL, SEXVAL, and TALENTVAL. If they match, we print out the values of the NAME, ADDRESS, and CITY fields of that folder. This is accomplished by the code:

```
while not(EOF(CABINET)) do
begin
    if ((CABINET^.MEDIUM = MEDIUMVAL)
        and (CABINET^.SEX = SEXVAL)
        and (CABINET^.TALENT = TALENTVAL)) then
        begin
            WRITELN(CABINET^.NAME);
            WRITELN('   ', CABINET^.ADDRESS, CABINET^.CITYSTA);
        end;
    get(CABINET);
end; (* while *)
```

Note that the statement get(CABINET) occurs after the first comparison and possible printing of FOLDER values. This reflects the convention in Pascal that the statement reset(CABINET) causes an immediate get (CABINET) to be done, thus fetching the first FOLDER in the file.

The complete program appears in Program 9-1.

Program 9-1. Retrieving Talent.

```
program TALENT(INPUT, CABINET);
(* ----------------------------------------------------------- *
 *       This program allows the user to search through the    *
 *  file CABINET looking for persons with various characteristics. *
 *  The entries in the file CABINET are FOLDERs, which are     *
 *  records. The fields of FOLDER are as follows: NAME,ADDRESS, *
 *  CITYSTA,MEDIUM,SEX,TALENT.                                 *
 *       The input to this program consists of values for the  *
 *  MEDIUM, SEX, and TALENT fields.                            *
 *       The output of the program is the name and address for *
 *  all FOLDERs that match the input field values.             *
 * ----------------------------------------------------------- *)
    const
       STRINGSIZE = 15;
    type
       STRING = packed array [1..STRINGSIZE] of CHAR;
       GIGS   = (STAGE, SCREEN, NIGHTCLUB, VAUDEVILLE,
                 TV,    RADIO,  RECORDING, POLITICS);
       SKILLS = (DRAMA,COMEDY,VOCALIST, DANCER,
                 INSTRUMENTALIST,       CAMPAIGNER);
       SEXES  = (MALE,FEMALE);
       FOLDER = record
                   NAME,ADDRESS,CITYSTA    : STRING;
                   MEDIUM  : GIGS;
                   SEX     : SEXES;
                   TALENT  : SKILLS;
                end;
    var
       CABINET   : file of FOLDER;
       MEDIUMVAL : GIGS;
       SEXVAL    : SEXES;
       TALENTVAL : SKILLS;

begin
   reset(CABINET);
   WRITE('Medium =');
   READ(MEDIUMVAL);
   WRITE('Talent =');
   READ(TALENTVAL);
   WRITE('Sex =');
   READ(SEXVAL);
```

Program 9-1. Continued.

```
    while not(EOF(CABINET)) do
    begin
       if ((CABINET^.MEDIUM = MEDIUMVAL)
             and (CABINET^.SEX = SEXVAL)
             and (CABINET^.TALENT = TALENTVAL)) then
          begin
             WRITELN(CABINET^.NAME);
             WRITELN('       ',CABINET^.ADDRESS,CABINET^.CITYSTA);
          end;
       get(CABINET);
    end; (* while *)
end.
```

Once again, we must now face up to the unpleasant (and idiotic) fact that standard Pascal does not sanction input or output of enumeration types via the procedures READ and WRITE. Consequently, we must adopt some sort of coding of the values of the enumeration types by either integers or characters. Let us code the types MEDIUM and GIGS by integers, enumerating the elements of the type in their given order; and let us code the elements of the type SEXES by the characters M and F, respectively. These are indeed quantities that we may input with READ. However, then we must convert from these codes to the corresponding values in the enumeration type. Consider MEDIUM first. We need a variable (for example, MEDIUMCODE) for READing in the code. After MEDIUMCODE is read in, we must convert it to an appropriate value for MEDIUMVAL. The most natural way to do this is to use a case statement. Thus we can obtain the desired MEDIUMVAL via the following code:

```
WRITE('Medium code (1-8) =');
READ(MEDIUMCODE);
case MEDIUMCODE of
     1  : MEDIUMVAL := STAGE;
     2  : MEDIUMVAL := SCREEN;
     3  : MEDIUMVAL := NIGHTCLUB;
     4  : MEDIUMVAL := TV;
     5  : MEDIUMVAL := VAUDEVILLE;
     6  : MEDIUMVAL := RADIO;
     7  : MEDIUMVAL := PLATTER;
     8  : MEDIUMVAL := POLITICS
   end; (* case *)
```

The corresponding code for obtaining SEXVAL is:

```
WRITE('Sex (M F)=');
READ(SEXCODE);
case SEXCODE of
    'M' : SEXVAL := MALE;
    'F' : SEXVAL := FEMALE;
   end; (* case *)
```

The complete text of this version of the program is presented in Program 9-2.

Program 9-2. TALENT with Coded Enumeration Types.

```
program TALENT(INPUT,CABINET)
(*  ------------------------------------------------------------ *
 *        This program allows the user to search through the file  *
 *  CABINET looking for persons with various characteristics. The  *
 *  entries in the file CABINET are FOLDERs, which are records     *
 *  with fields NAME,ADDRESS, CITY,MEDIUM,SEX,TALENT. The first    *
 *  three are STRING types. The last three are enumeration types.  *
 *        Since standard Pascal does not provide for direct I-O of *
 *  enumeration types, they must be coded. The I-O  codes for      *
 *  the corresponding types are as follows:                        *
 *        GIGS:                                                     *
 *            1 - stage    2 - screen     3 - nightclub            *
 *            4 - TV       5 - vaudeville 6 - radio                 *
 *            7 - recording 8 - politics                           *
 *        SEX:                                                      *
 *            F - female   M - male                                *
 *        SKILLS:                                                   *
 *            1 - drama    2 - comedy     3 - singer               *
 *            4 - dancer   5 - instrument 6 - campaigning          *
 *        The input to this program consists of values for the     *
 *  MEDIUM, SEX, and TALENT fields. The program then searches      *
 *  through the file CABINET looking for all FOLDERs that          *
 *  match these field values.                                      *
 *        The output of the program is the name and address for    *
 *  all FOLDERs that match the input field values.                 *
 *  ------------------------------------------------------------ *)
    const
       STRINGSIZE = 15;
    type
       STRING = packed array [1..STRINGSIZE] of CHAR;
       GIGS   = (STAGE, SCREEN, NIGHTCLUB, VAUDEVILLE,
                 TV,    RADIO,   RECORDING, POLITICS);
       SKILLS = (DRAMA,COMEDY,VOCALIST, DANCER,
                 INSTRUMENTALIST,        CAMPAIGNER);
       SEXES  = (MALE, FEMALE);
       FOLDER = record
                   NAME,ADDRESS,CITY   : STRING;
                   MEDIUM : GIGS;
                   SEX    : SEXES;
                   TALENT : SKILLS;
                end;
```

Program 9-2. Continued.

```
    var
        CABINET                         : file of FOLDER;
        MEDIUMCODE,TALENTCODE           : integer;
        SEXCODE                         : CHAR;
        MEDIUMVAL                       : GIGS;
        SEXVAL                          : SEXES;
        TALENTVAL                       : SKILLS;
begin
    reset(CABINET);

    WRITE('Medium code (1-8) =');
    READ(MEDIUMCODE);
    case MEDIUMCODE of
        1  : MEDIUMVAL := STAGE;
        2  : MEDIUMVAL := SCREEN;
        3  : MEDIUMVAL := NIGHTCLUB;
        4  : MEDIUMVAL := TV;
        5  : MEDIUMVAL := VAUDEVILLE;
        6  : MEDIUMVAL := RADIO;
        7  : MEDIUMVAL := RECORDING;
        8  : MEDIUMVAL := POLITICS;
    end; (* case *)

    WRITE('Talent code (1-6) =');
    READ(TALENTCODE);
    case TALENTCODE of
        1  : TALENTVAL := DRAMA;
        2  : TALENTVAL := COMEDY;
        3  : TALENTVAL := VOCALIST;
        4  : TALENTVAL := DANCER;
        5  : TALENTVAL := INSTRUMENTALIST;
        6  : TALENTVAL := CAMPAIGNER;
    end; (* case *)

    WRITE('Sex (M F) =');
    READ(SEXCODE);
    case SEXCODE of
        'M' : SEXVAL := MALE;
        'F' : SEXVAL := FEMALE
    end; (* case *)
```

Program 9-2.   Continued.

```
while not(EOF(CABINET)) do
begin
    if ((CABINET^.MEDIUM = MEDIUMVAL)
        and (CABINET^.SEX = SEXVAL)
        and (CABINET^.TALENT = TALENTVAL)) then
      begin
      WRITELN(CABINET^.NAME);
      WRITELN('          ',CABINET^.ADDRESS,CABINET^.CITY);
      end;

    get(CABINET);
  end; (* while *)
end.
```

This certainly provides us with a method of rummaging about in the agent's file CABINET. The only difficulty is that we have not bothered to put anything there yet! What we need is a program to obtain the information for the FOLDERs, construct the folders, and to place them into the file CABINET. We will construct such a program called MAKECABINET. It will be used to construct the first file CABINET. A program for adding FOLDERs to an already existing file CABINET is described in Exercise 9-3.

For each folder, the program will need to obtain the person's NAME, ADDRESS, CITY, MEDIUM, SEX, and TALENT. Obtaining the latter three can be done using the coding methods of the program TALENT. However, we must also obtain the values of NAME, ADDRESS, and CITY. These are STRINGS, which in reality are packed arrays of CHAR. Though we may output these with the WRITE statement, the READ statement does not allow us to input them. So we must build our own machinery for reading them in.

Our goal is to be able to call a procedure, such as READSTRING, and as a result of this call, find that a STRING of CHARacters has been read into a STRING variable. Thus at the right time, we would like to call READSTRING and find that a name has been read into NEXTFOLDER. NAME. Then by calling READSTRING again, we would find that an address has been read into NEXTFOLDER.ADDRESS; and with a third call of READSTRING, we would find that a city has been read into NEXTFOLDER.CITY. Obviously, if we are to be able to do this, we must be able to specify to READSTRING which variable it is to read the CHARacters into. Such a facility is provided by the use of variable parameters, which we discussed at the end of Chapter 7. Thus the declaration of the procedure READSTRING should begin with

```
procedure READSTRING( var GOALSTRING : STRING)
```

Then the three calls of READSTRING we described above would be expressed as:

```
READSTRING(NEXTFOLDER.NAME);
READSTRING(NEXTFOLDER.ADDRESS);
READSTRING(NEXTFOLDER.CITY)
```

Whatever code we actually write for the body of READSTRING, the effect of these codes will be as though the actual variable (for example, NEXTFOLDER.NAME) was substituted for GOALSTRING throughout the body of READSTRING and then the body was executed.

Now we must set about designing the body of READSTRING. What is desired is this: the procedure will input characters from the current input line until it has either filled the array GOALSTRING or read to the end of the input line. If it reaches the end of the input line before it reaches the end of the array GOALSTRING, it will fill the remaining portion of GOALSTRING with blanks. Thus the top-level design of READSTRING can be presented as follows:

```
procedure READSTRING( var GOALSTRING : STRING);
begin
```
   Input characters into the array GOALSTRING until either GOALSTRING is filled or the end of the input line is reached;

   If GOALSTRING is not filled, fill it out with blanks;
```
end; (* READSTRING *)
```

Probably the easiest way to accomplish these acts is to keep track of the number of characters that have been read. Since GOALSTRING will accept STRINGSIZE many CHARacters, we can easily test whether or not we have filled GOALSTRING. The actual process of reading in a character is similar to that in the program NOTETAKER (Chapter 6). You will recall that we are presuming the input data for the FOLDERs will come from the standard file INPUT. Thus the procedure READSTRING may now be presented:

```
procedure READSTRING(var GOALSTRING : STRING);
var
      COUNT  : integer;
begin
   COUNT := 1;
   while ((COUNT <= STRINGSIZE) and not(EOLN)) do
      begin
         READ(GOALSTRING[COUNT]);
         COUNT := COUNT + 1;
      end;

   if COUNT < STRINGSIZE then
      for COUNT := COUNT to STRINGSIZE do
         GOALSTRING[COUNT] := ' ';
   READLN;
end; (* READSTRING *)
```

Now we may combine this procedure with the coded input methods in TALENT to produce the complete program for MAKE-CABINET shown in Program 9-3.

Program 9-3.   A Program for Constructing a File CABINET

```
program MAKECABINET(INPUT, CABINET);
(*  ------------------------------------------------------------ *
 *       This program constructs the file CABINET to be used     *
 *  by the program TALENT. The details of encoding enumeration   *
 *  types are presented in the text.                             *
 *       The inputs to the program are the values for the fields *
 *  of the FOLDERs to be entered in the CABINET. The records to  *
 *  be input are assumed to be in the standard file INPUT with   *
 *  each field on its own line.                                  *
 *       The output of the program is the file CABINET with      *
 *  the appropriate records inserted.                            *
 *       The procedure READSTRING inputs a line of characters    *
 *  into the variable GOALSTRING. If the input line is longer than *
 *  STRINGSIZE, the input line is truncated. If the input line is *
 *  shorter than STRINGSIZE, GOALSTRING is padded with blanks.   *
 *  ------------------------------------------------------------ *)
    const
        STRINGSIZE = 15;

    type
        STRING = packed array [1..STRINGSIZE] of CHAR;
        GIGS   = (STAGE,SCREEN,NIGHTCLUB,VAUDEVILLE,
                    TV,   RADIO, RECORDING,POLITICS);
        SKILLS = (DRAMA,COMEDY,VOCALIST, DANCER,
                    INSTRUMENTALIST,      CAMPAIGNER);
        SEXES  = (MALE,FEMALE);
        FOLDER = record
                    NAME, ADDRESS, CITY    : STRING;
                    MEDIUM  : GIGS;
                    SEX     : SEXES;
                    TALENT  : SKILLS;
                 end;

    var
        CABINET : file of FOLDER;
        NEXTFOLDER : FOLDER;
        MEDIUMCODE,TALENTCODE : integer;
        SEXCODE : CHAR;
```

Program 9-3.   Continued.

```
procedure READSTRING(var GOALSTRING : STRING);
    var
        COUNT : integer;
    begin
      COUNT := 1;
      while ((COUNT <= STRINGSIZE) and not(EOLN)) do
          begin
             READ(GOALSTRING[COUNT]);
             COUNT := COUNT + 1;
          end;
      if COUNT < STRINGSIZE then
          for COUNT := COUNT to STRINGSIZE do
             GOALSTRING[COUNT] := ' ';
      READLN;
    end; (* READSTRING *)

begin  (* Main Program *)
    repeat
      READSTRING(NEXTFOLDER.NAME);
      READSTRING(NEXTFOLDER.ADDRESS);
      READSTRING(NEXTFOLDER.CITYSTA);

      READ(MEDIUMCODE);
      case MEDIUMCODE of
          1  : NEXTFOLDER.MEDIUM := STAGE;
          2  : NEXTFOLDER.MEDIUM := SCREEN;
          3  : NEXTFOLDER.MEDIUM := NIGHTCLUB;
          4  : NEXTFOLDER.MEDIUM := TV;
          5  : NEXTFOLDER.MEDIUM := VAUDEVILLE;
          6  : NEXTFOLDER.MEDIUM := RADIO;
          7  : NEXTFOLDER.MEDIUM := RECORDING;
          8  : NEXTFOLDER.MEDIUM := POLITICS;
      end; (* case *)

      READ(TALENTCODE);
      case TALENTCODE of
          1  : NEXTFOLDER.TALENT := DRAMA;
          2  : NEXTFOLDER.TALENT := COMEDY;
          3  : NEXTFOLDER.TALENT := VOCALIST;
          4  : NEXTFOLDER.TALENT := DANCER;
          5  : NEXTFOLDER.TALENT := INSTRUMENTALIST;
          6  : NEXTFOLDER.TALENT := CAMPAIGNER;
      end; (* case *)
```

Program 9-3. Continued.

```
    READ(SEXCODE);
    case SEXCODE of
            'M' : NEXTFOLDER^ .SEX := MALE;
            'F' : NEXTFOLDER^ .SEX := FEMALE;
    end; (* case *)

    CABINET^ := NEXTFOLDER;
    put(CABINET);
  until  EOF;
end.
```

Exercises

Exercise 9-1 Design record types suitable for describing the following:

a) Inventory records for your local drugstore.
b) Library cards at your local library.

Exercise 9-2 Construct a program DISPLAYCABINET that will print out the entire contents of the file CABINET.

Exercise 9-3 Design a program ADDTOCABINET that will add FOLDERs to an already existing file CABINET. (Hint: The statement REWRITE always blanks the file it is applied to. Therefore, one must first read CABINET over to a temporary file TEMPCAB and then read TEMPCAB back over into CABINET. At this point the file window is at the end of the already existing CABINET ready to add more FOLDERs at the end.)

Exercise 9-4 Given the enumeration types SUITS and CARDS as in Exercise 8-7, a reasonable representation of cards is

```
CARD = record
          SUTE : SUITS;
          FACEV: CARDS;
       end
```

Using this representation, revise the program DEALER of Exercise 8-7. In particular, note that the hands can now be realized as:

```
NORTH,SOUTH,EAST,WEST : array[1..13] of CARD
```

Chapter Ten

Elegant Discourse:
Program Design Methodology

We have now studied the major elements of Pascal and have used them in a variety of programming conversations. The time has come for us to think a bit about the quality of these conversations. In particular, we must consider methods of design and procedures that can lead to elegant and lucid programs. The topics in this chapter will include

- Top down development of structured programs.
- Programming style.

10.1   Top-Down Design

The key to the successful solution of any problem, be it simple and small or large and complex, is careful thought and planning before taking a single step. This approach, however, takes real strength of character. When large or complicated programming problems rear their heads, a common reaction is total panic: it's gotta be done tomorrow! (If not yesterday!) Keeping your cool becomes especially important (particularly when everyone else is losing theirs). Instead of starting to sling code left and right, it is far better to clear your desk and your mind, get a cup of coffee or coke or whatever you drink, put your feet up, and think.

The first thought that you ought to seriously entertain is:

"Just what is the problem anyway?"

Rarely is the first statement of a problem anywhere near a correct and complete statement of what must be accomplished. For this reason alone, you should avoid all thought of code at first. What good does it do you to cook up a batch of code for the wrong problem? In all likelihood, fast code slinging will end up taking you more time overall than cautious preliminary thinking.

At any rate, the first step is to think carefully through the nature of the problem. In particular, you must get the problem completely defined. This may take some painful thought on your part and may necessitate discussions with a boss or intended users of your program. But it is absolutely necessary: you have no hope of building a correct program if you don't know precisely what it is you must build.

In the vast majority of problems, a precise definition involves a careful specification of all the inputs and outputs for the program together with an exact specification of the relationships between the inputs and outputs. Once this is at hand, one can proceed with a careful *top-down* design procedure.

At its upper levels, the top-down methodology is not at all unique to the design of computer programs: it can be profitably employed in the design of complex manual and management systems or the design of complex physical devices. One begins with the big picture, trying to see the system or problem as a whole, with details totally suppressed. Then one gradually divides this large whole into natural interrelated components or subproblems. If these components are themselves complex, the process of subdivision is repeated again with them, and so on, until finally one arrives at simple understandable subproblems that are amenable to direct solution. The analysis, however, has shown how these subproblems relate to one another, so that once the subproblems are solved, the solutions are easily combined·into a solution of the parent problem. Thus, in essence, the method of top-down design is simply the method of "divide and conquer," which we have already discussed (Chapter 8).

The essential points then in using a top-down design methodology are these:

1. *Design in levels with each successive level being a refinement of the last level above.* At each level except the lowest, there will be "modules" or "components" that are as yet unelaborated. You will know what these modules must do to fulfill their role in the design at the current level. But you will not yet have worked out how they are to accomplish their tasks. Working this out is begun at the next level of refinement following the present one.

2. *At the upper levels, the design should be independent of any particular programming language.* Thus most of the design at this point should be expressed in clear and precise English, perhaps together with simple control "skeletons" such as if-then-else or repeat-until.

3. *Relationships between modules should be precise at any level.* Even at the upper level where much of the description is in English, it should be exact and clear what the arguments and outputs of any module are, what it expects to be true about its inputs, and what it will guarantee to be true about its outputs. Given this level of precision and formality, the refinement of the modules at lower levels will not cause revisions of the relationships between the modules at the upper levels.

This provides a general description of a methodology that can be very successful in developing elegant, lucid, and correct programs. Like all general descriptions, it is best supplemented with a good example. We do that in the next section.

10.2 Pretty Comments

You probably have noticed the pretty boxed form in which comments in programs have been presented. (How could you miss!) Let us use our methodology to develop a program which will transform ugly old unboxed comments into pretty boxed comments. It should, of course, leave the rest of the program alone. Thus, for example, the program DOUBLING in Chapter 4 might have originally appeared as shown in Figure 10-1. Its transformed version appears in Figure 10-2.

```
program DOUBLING;
(*   This program takes two real number inputs: STARTINGAMOUNT and GOALAMOUNT.
It assumes that STARTINGAMOUNT is to be doubled, redoubled, and so on, every YEAR.
   The output of the program is the number of YEARs of such doubling and redoubling
until the original STARTINGAMOUNT has grown at least as large as the GOALAMOUNT.
   var
       YEAR : INTEGER;
       STARTINGAMOUNT, GOALAMOUNT, CURRENTVALUE : real;
begin
   WRITE('STARTING AMOUNT =')
   READ(STARTINGAMOUNT);

   WRITE('GOAL AMOUNT =')
   READ(GOALAMOUNT);

   YEAR := 0;
   CURRENTVALUE := STARTINGAMOUNT;

   while CURRENTVALUE < GOALAMOUNT do
       begin   (* One YEAR's doubling *)
           CURRENTVALUE := CURRENTVALUE * 2;
           YEAR := YEAR + 1;
       end;

   WRITELN('DOUBLING EVERY YEAR, $',   STARTINGAMOUNT:8:2,
           ' WILL REACH OR EXCEED $', GOALAMOUNT:8:2,
           ' AFTER ',     YEAR:4,       'YEARS. '     );

end.
```

Figure 10-1. The Program DOUBLING: Original Form.

```
program DOUBLING;
(* ----------------------------------------------------------- *
 *        This program takes two real number inputs:            *
 *  STARTINGAMOUNT and GOALAMOUNT. It assumes that STARTINGAMOUNT *
 *  is to be doubled, redoubled, and so on, every YEAR.          *
 *        The output of the program is the number of YEARs of such *
 *  doubling and redoubling until the original STARTINGAMOUNT    *
 *  has grown at least as large as the GOALAMOUNT.               *
 *  ----------------------------------------------------------- *)
    var
       YEAR : INTEGER;
       STARTINGAMOUNT, GOALAMOUNT, CURRENTVALUE : real;
begin
    WRITE('STARTING AMOUNT =');
    READ(STARTINGAMOUNT);

    WRITE('GOAL AMOUNT =');
    READ(GOALAMOUNT);

    YEAR := 0;
    CURRENTVALUE := STARTINGAMOUNT;

    while CURRENTVALUE < GOALAMOUNT do
          begin  (* One YEAR's doubling *)
             CURRENTVALUE := CURRENTVALUE * 2;
             YEAR := YEAR + 1;
          end;

    WRITELN('DOUBLING EVERY YEAR, $',  STARTINGAMOUNT:8:2,
            ' WILL REACH OR EXCEED $', GOALAMOUNT:8:2,
            ' AFTER ',    YEAR:4,      'YEARS.'    );

end.
```

Figure 10-2. The Program DOUBLING Transformed.

This example suggests what our program will and won't do:

1. It will transform comments whose opening comment symbol "(*" appears at the left margin of the page.

2. It will not transform a comment whose opening "(*" does not occur at the left margin.

3. It does not affect the program text.

Examining Figure 10-2 further, we see that it acts on the transformed comments as follows:

1. The top and bottom lines of the output are special "box lines."

2. All other lines of the output comment start with space, asterisk, space, followed by the text on that line, and terminate with a space and an asterisk.

3. If an input line other than the first begins with a blank, a new output line is started.

4. Output lines are "filled" in the sense that as many words from the input comment are put on one outline as will fit while maintaining indenting and so forth.

5. Any blank input line is output as a blank line with appropriate asterisks as given above.

6. With one exception, input blanks are transmitted as is to the output comment.

7. The exception to the "as is" transmission of blanks is this: if a blank not occurring at the beginning of an input line would otherwise be placed at the start of an output line, it is skipped entirely.

The fact that our specifications for the program naturally break down into two parts suggests that our design process can proceed similarly. That is, we may first design the top level of the program to reflect the first part of the specifications and then later incorporate the second part as we refine the original top-level design.

In order to recognize comments that start at the left-hand side of the page in the source file, it makes sense to process the source file line by line. Of course, whenever we discover the start of a comment at the left margin, we will process the comment in its entirety. Thus a first outline for our program is as follows:

```
program COMMENT;
(*  ------------------------------------------------------------  *
 *        This program transforms ordinary comments in Pascal     *
 *   programs into boxed comments. It only transforms those       *
 *   comments whose opening symbol is at the far left side of     *
 *   the line on which they begin. It leaves all other comments,  *
 *   as well as the program proper, untouched.                    *
 *        The input is the original source Pascal program.        *
 *        The output is the transformed program.                  *
 *  ------------------------------------------------------------ *)
begin
    while Lines remain in source file do
        if Next line is the start of a comment to be boxed then
            Box up the entire comment
        else
            Transfer line from source to output without change
end.
```

Figure 10-3. Top-level Outline of COMMENT.

This outline breaks down the work into five parts:

1. Determining the source and destination files.
2. Determining at any point in the processing whether or not any lines remain in the source file.
3. Determining whether or not a given line is the first line of a comment that must be boxed.
4. Boxing such a comment.
5. Transferring a line unaltered from the source file to the destination file.

With regard to the source and destination files, the simplest decision to make is to choose them to be the standard files INPUT and OUTPUT. Given this decision, and assuming that the overall processing really is line by line, then the question as to whether or not there are any lines remaining in the file INPUT is answered by the Boolean expression

```
not(EOF(INPUT))
```

The question as to whether or not a given line is the beginning of a comment will presumably be answered by a Boolean function that we will call COMMENTSTART. The process of carrying out the boxing up of a comment will be effected by a procedure called BOXCOMMENT, while the job of transferring a line unaltered from INPUT to OUTPUT will be carried out by a procedure called TRANSFER. However the procedure BOXCOMMENT comes to work, it will operate under the following assumptions: when it is called in the program, the file window INPUT^ will be positioned looking at the character immediately after the symbol that opens the comment, and when BOXCOMMENT finishes running, the file window INPUT^ will be positioned looking at the character immediately following the symbol which closes the comment. Note that for our purposes here, we will treat the expression "(*" as one single symbol (even though it is made up of two typewriter symbols). Similarly, "*)" is also treated as a single symbol. Given these decisions, our first refinement of the original outline of COMMENT now appears in Figure 10-4.

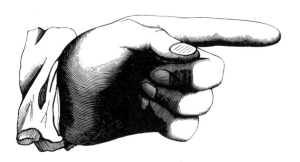

```
program COMMENT(INPUT,OUTPUT);
(*  --------------------------------------------------------------  *
 *         This program transforms ordinary comments in Pascal    *
 *  programs into boxed comments, filling out the lines in the box *
 *  where appropriate. It only transforms those comments whose    *
 *  opening symbol is at the far left side of the line on which   *
 *  they begin. It leaves all other comments, and the program     *
 *  proper, untouched. It also attempts to preserve the           *
 *  indenting and blank line structure of the original comment.   *
 *         The input is the original source program.              *
 *         The output is the transformed program.                 *
 *         The principal procedure is BOXCOMMENT. This procedure  *
 *  expects to be called when the INPUT file window is "near"     *
 *  the beginning of a comment that must be boxed. It reads       *
 *  through this entire comment, outputting the properly boxed    *
 *  form to the file OUTPUT. When the procedure finishes running, *
 *  the INPUT file window is positioned after the close of        *
 *  the comment just processed.                                   *
 *  --------------------------------------------------------------  *)
    function COMMENTSTART : BOOLEAN;
    begin
        Body of the function
    end; (* COMMENTSTART *)

    procedure BOXCOMMENT;
    begin
        Body of the procedure
    end; (* BOXCOMMENT *)

    procedure TRANSFER;
    begin
        Body of the procedure
    end; (* TRANSFER *)

begin
    while not(EOF(INPUT)) do
        if COMMENTSTART then
            BOXCOMMENT
        else
            TRANSFER
end.
```

Figure 10-4. First Refinement of COMMENT.

We must now develop the function COMMENTSTART together with the two procedures BOXCOMMENT and TRANSFER. Let us begin with the function COMMENTSTART. When it is called, it will expect the file window INPUT^ to be positioned looking at the first character on the present input line. The function must determine whether or not the first two symbols of the line are "(" and "*" in that order. Thus it must read the first character into an appropriate variable; it can then use the file window INPUT^ to look at the second character. Suppose that FIRSTCHAR is declared to be of type CHAR and the following constant definitions have been made:

```
LEFTPAREN = '(';
ASTERISK  = '*'
```

Then the statement READ(INPUT,FIRSTCHAR) will have the effect of reading a character into the variable FIRSTCHAR; presumably this will be the very first character of a given input line. Then the Boolean expression

```
((FIRSTCHAR = LEFTPAREN) and (INPUT^ = ASTERISK))
```

will be true precisely when the given input line begins with the symbol "(*". Thus in this case, the value of the function should be TRUE; otherwise, it will be FALSE.

However, at this point we must consider the actions that will occur in these two cases. When COMMENTSTART returns value FALSE, the procedure TRANSFER will run. It has no arguments, and so presumably it will transfer all the characters from the given input line to OUTPUT. However, one of the characters of the given input line has already been read in and is not available to TRANSFER, namely, the very first character that was read into FIRSTCHAR. Thus COMMENTSTART must see to it that this character gets sent to the file OUTPUT before it returns its value and lets TRANSFER start running. Therefore, in case the Boolean expression above returns FALSE, COMMENTSTART must execute

```
WRITE(OUTPUT,FIRSTCHAR)
```

A similar problem faces us in case the Boolean expression returns true. In that case, the procedure BOXCOMMENT will begin running. However, when it starts up, it expects the file window INPUT^ to be looking at the first character following the opening comment symbol "(*". Since this symbol is really made up of two characters, at this point the file window INPUT^ will be looking at the "*" in this comment symbol. Thus in this case we must execute another READ statement to advance the file window one character:

    READ(INPUT,FIRSTCHAR)

With these observations, we may now completely design COMMENT-START, as show in Figure 10-5.

```
function COMMENTSTART : BOOLEAN;
      var
         FIRSTCHAR : CHAR;
    begin
      READ(INPUT,FIRSTCHAR);
      if ((FIRSTCHAR = LEFTPAREN) and (INPUT^ = ASTERISK)) then
         begin
            COMMENTSTART := TRUE;
            READ(INPUT,FIRSTCHAR)
         end
      else
         begin
            COMMENTSTART := FALSE;
            WRITE(OUTPUT,FIRSTCHAR);
         end
    end; (* COMMENTSTART *)
```

Figure 10-5. The Function COMMENTSTART.

Now consider the procedure TRANSFER. When it is called, it expects to transfer the remainder of the current input line, character by character – as is to the file OUTPUT. Its operation is quite similar to that of the revised version of the program NOTETAKER. These procedures may be combined to produce the next refinement of COMMENT, as shown in Figure 10-6.

Figure 10-6. Second Refinement of COMMENT.

```
program COMMENT(INPUT,OUTPUT);
(*  -----------------------------------------------------------  *
 *                                                               *
 *         This program transforms ordinary comments in Pascal   *
 *   programs into boxed comments, filling out the lines in the box *
 *   where appropriate. It only transforms those comments whose  *
 *   opening symbol is at the far left side of the line on which *
 *   they begin. It leaves all other comments, and the program   *
 *   proper, untouched. It also attempts to preserve the         *
 *   indenting and blank line structure of the original comment. *
 *         The input is the original source program.             *
 *         The output is the transformed program.                *
 *         The principal procedure is BOXCOMMENT. This procedure *
 *   expects to be called when the INPUT file window is "near"   *
 *   the beginning of a comment that must be boxed. It reads     *
 *   through this entire comment, outputting the properly boxed  *
 *   form to the file OUTPUT. When the procedure finishes running, *
 *   the INPUT file window is positioned after the close of      *
 *   the comment just processed.                                 *
 *  -----------------------------------------------------------  *)
    const
      LEFTPAREN = '(';
      ASTERISK  = '*';

    function COMMENTSTART : BOOLEAN;
      var
        FIRSTCHAR : CHAR;
    begin
      READ(INPUT,FIRSTCHAR);
      if ((FIRSTCHAR = LEFTPAREN) and (INPUT^ = ASTERISK)) then
          begin
            COMMENTSTART := TRUE;
            READ(INPUT,FIRSTCHAR)
          end
      else
          begin
            COMMENTSTART := FALSE;
            WRITE(OUTPUT,FIRSTCHAR);
          end
    end; (* COMMENTSTART *)
```

Figure 10-6. Continued.

```
procedure BOXCOMMENT;
begin
    Body of the procedure
end; (* BOXCOMMENT *)

procedure TRANSFER;
    var LETTER : CHAR;
begin
    while (not(EOF(INPUT)) and not(EOLN(INPUT))) do
    begin
        READ(INPUT,LETTER);
        WRITE(OUTPUT,LETTER)
    end;

    if not(EOF(INPUT) then
        READLN(INPUT);

    WRITELN(OUTPUT)
end; (* TRANSFER *)

begin  (* Main Program *)
    while not(EOF(INPUT)) do
        if COMMENTSTART then
            BOXCOMMENT
        else
            TRANSFER
end.
```

As Figure 10-6 shows, our program now meets the first group of requirements in our list. In the process of refining the procedure BOXCOMMENT, we must satisfy the second group of requirements. So let us begin this task.

The first thing BOXCOMMENT must do is print the top line of the comment box. Then, line by line, it must process the input comment into the output form. And finally, when this processing is complete, it must print the bottom line of the comment box. One simple way to keep track of whether or not the processing is complete is to use a Boolean variable, such as DONE. This is initially set to FALSE, and then some portion of the input processing resets it to TRUE when the closing comment symbol of the input comment is encountered. Finally, as our requirements indicate, the very first line of the input comment may be treated somewhat differently from the rest of the input lines; therefore, it makes sense to process it separately. With these observations in mind, the first outline of BOXCOMMENT is presented in Figure 10-7.

```
procedure BOXCOMMENT;
    var
        DONE : BOOLEAN;
        Other necessary variables;
    begin
        DONE := FALSE;
        Other necessary initialization;
        Print top line of comment box;

        Process first input line;

        while not(DONE) do
            begin
                Process next input line;
                if not(DONE) then
                    READLN(INPUT);
            end;

        Print bottom line of box;
    end; (* BOXCOMMENT *)
```

Figure 10-7. First Outline of Procedure BOXCOMMENT.

Printing the top line of the comment box is quite straightforward. First the symbol "(*" must be printed, followed by the appropriate number of hyphens (-), and then a final asterisk must be printed. To determine just how many hyphens to print, we must decide how wide the comment boxes are to be. Those that have been constructed in our programs thus far have been 60 characters across. Consequently, let us add the following constant definitions to the main program:

```
COMMENTWIDTH = 60;
HYPHEN       = '-';
COMMENTOPEN  = '(*';
COMMENTCLOSE = '*)'
```

Printing the bottom line of the comment box is similarly easy. The procedures PRINTTOPLINE and PRINTBOTTOMLINE are presented in Figure 10-10.

This leaves us with the routines for processing the input lines. We have drawn a distinction between processing the first input comment line and processing the rest. But this distinction is minor; that is, if the very first input line begins with a space, we will not start a new output line. Otherwise, as far as our requirements are concerned, the processing will be the same. So it would appear that one way to deal with this difference would be to utilize a Boolean variable STARTING to indicate whether or not the line about to be processed is the very first input line. Then the same processing routine, PROCESSINPUTLINE, can be used for both circumstances. It will simply vary its activity depending on the value of STARTING. Thus the main body of BOXCOMMENT is presented in Figure 10-8.

```
begin  (* Body of BOXCOMMENT *)
   DONE := FALSE;
   Other necessary initialization;
   PRINTTOPLINE;

   STARTING := TRUE;
   PROCESSINPUTLINE;
   STARTING := FALSE;

   while not(DONE) do
   begin
      PROCESSINPUTLINE;
      if not(DONE) then
         READLN(INPUT);
   end;

   PRINTBOTTOMLINE
end; (* BOXCOMMENT *)
```

Figure 10-8. First Refinement of BOXCOMMENT.

By the use of our systematic, top-down strategy, we have delayed until now the consideration of just how the lines of the output comment will be constructed. This delay is not at all frivolous: we have been able to strip away and deal with other important considerations and thus at the present point, we have no other problems to distract us.

So now let us focus on the output lines. Of course, in general there will not be a direct correspondence between the input lines and the output lines. (Otherwise, we would not be writing this program!) Thus the processing of input lines must amount to getting successive words and spaces from the input lines, using them to build a model or picture of an output line, and (as each output line is filled) sending it off to the OUTPUT file. What data structure can we use for building up the pictures of the output line? Perhaps the most natural is an array[1..COMMENTWIDTH] of CHAR. Then as we build the output line, we will put characters in exactly the positions we want them to appear in the printed OUTPUT form. Suppose we make the declaration:

```
OUTPUTLINE : array[1..COMMENTWIDTH] of CHAR
```

As we go about processing the input line, we will need a variable to keep track of our present position in OUTPUTLINE to tell us the next unused location. Suppose we declare

```
LINEINDEX : 1..COMMENTWIDTH
```

for this.

A small routine will begin the construction of OUTPUTLINE as indicated above appears in Figure 10-9.

```
procedure STARTOUTPUTLINE;
begin
    OUTPUTLINE[1] := SPACE;
    OUTPUTLINE[2] := ASTERISK;
    OUTPUTLINE[3] := SPACE;

    OUTPUTLINE[COMMENTWIDTH-1] := SPACE;
    OUTPUTLINE[COMMENTWIDTH]   := ASTERISK;
end; (* STARTOUTPUTLINE *)
```

Figure 10-9.   A Procedure to Initialize OUTPUTLINE.

Using these considerations, we may complete the refinement of BOXCOMMENT, with the exception of PROCESSINPUTLINE, as shown in Figure 10-10.

Figure 10-10. Refinement of BOXCOMMENT

```
procedure BOXCOMMENT;
    var
        DONE,STARTING : BOOLEAN;
        OUTPUTLINE    : array[1..COMMENTWIDTH] of CHAR;
        LINEINDEX     : 1..COMMENTWIDTH;

    procedure PRINTTOPLINE;
        var
            COUNTER : 1..COMMENTWIDTH;
    begin
        WRITE(OUTPUT,COMMENTOPEN);
        for COUNTER := 3 to COMMENTWIDTH-1 do
            WRITE(OUTPUT,HYPHEN);
        WRITELN(OUTPUT,ASTERISK)
    end; (* PRINTTOPLINE) *)

    procedure PRINTBOTTOMLINE;
        var
            COUNTER : 1..COMMENTWIDTH;
    begin
        WRITE(OUTPUT,SPACE,ASTERISK);
        for COUNTER := 3 to COMMENTWIDTH-1 do
            WRITE(OUTPUT,HYPHEN);
        WRITELN(OUTPUT,COMMENTCLOSE)
    end; (* PRINTBOTTOMLINE *)

    procedure STARTOUTPUTLINE;
    begin
        OUTPUTLINE[1] := SPACE;
        OUTPUTLINE[2] := ASTERISK;
        OUTPUTLINE[3] := SPACE;

        OUTPUTLINE[COMMENTWIDTH-1] := SPACE;
        OUTPUTLINE[COMMENTWIDTH]   := ASTERISK;
    end; (* STARTOUTPUTLINE *)

    procedure PROCESSINPUTLINE;
    begin
        Body of the procedure;
    end; (* PROCESSINPUTLINE *)
```

Figure 10-10.   Continued.

```
begin  (* Main Program *)
    DONE := FALSE;
    STARTOUTPUTLINE;
    LINEINDEX := 4;

    PRINTTOPLINE;

    STARTING := TRUE;
    PROCESSINPUTLINE;
    STARTING := FALSE;

    while not(DONE) do
    begin
        PROCESSINPUTLINE;
        if not(DONE) then
            READLN(INPUT);
    end;

    PRINTBOTTOMLINE
end;  (* BOXCOMMENT *)
```

Let us now consider the action of PROCESSINPUTLINE. First, it must distinguish between blank input lines and input lines containing characters. This is described in the following fragment:

```
if Input line is blank then
    begin
        Terminate & fill OUTPUTLINE & send it to OUTPUT file;
        Print blank line on OUTPUT file;
        Position file window at beginning of next line
    end
else...
```

When the line is not blank, we will, of course, immediately obtain the first character of the line. If this character is a SPACE and if we are not processing the very first line, we must begin a new output line. Consequently, we may extend the fragmentary outline of PROCESS-INPUTLINE as follows:

```
if Input line is blank then
  begin
    Terminate & fill OUTPUTLINE & send it to OUTPUT file;
    Print blank line on OUTPUT file;
    Position file window at beginning of next line
  end
else
begin
    Get the leading character from the input line;
    if (The character is SPACE) and not(STARTING) then
      begin
        Terminate & fill out OUTPUTLINE & send it to OUTPUT;
        OUTPUTLINE[4] := The character just read;
        LINEINDEX := 5;
        Continue processing the rest of the input line
      end
    else ...
      ...
end
```

In the remaining case, either the first character is not a SPACE or
it is a SPACE and we are indeed processing the first line of the input
comment. If the character is not a SPACE, we must obtain (from the
input line) the complete word that the character begins. Thus, we may
extend the outline for PROCESSINPUT as follows:

```
if Input line is blank then
  begin
    Terminate & fill OUTPUTLINE & send it to OUTPUT file;
    Print blank line on OUTPUT file;
    Position file window at beginning of next line
  end
else
begin
  Get the leading character from the input line;
  if (The character is SPACE) and not(STARTING) then
    begin
      Terminate & fill out OUTPUTLINE & send it to OUTPUT;
      OUTPUTLINE[4]  := The character just read;
      LINEINDEX      := 5;
      Continue processing the rest of the input line
    end
  else
    begin
      Get word beginning with the character just read;
      if Word doesn't fit in OUTPUTLINE then
        Terminate & fill OUTPUTLINE, send it to OUTPUT
            file, & start new OUTPUTLINE;
      Insert the word in OUTPUTLINE;
      if DONE then
        Terminate & fill OUTPUTLINE, & send to OUTPUT file
      else
        Continue processing the input line
    end
end
```

Since we will be reading characters, we need a variable to accomplish this. Let us use NEXTCHARACTER. We will also need a method of reading words from the input line. Given the way we have already chosen to represent lines by arrays, it is natural to do the same for individual words. We will, therefore, use WORD as an array of CHAR. And we might as well make it

```
WORD : array[1..COMMENTWIDTH] of CHAR
```

to minimize the restrictions we must impose. Just as with our OUTPUTLINE, we will need a variable, such as WORDINDEX, to keep track of our current position in WORD.

Finally, let us choose some names for the basic processes that occur in this outline. SHIPOUTPUTLINE will be the procedure that terminates construction of the current OUTPUTLINE, fills the unused portions with blanks, sends it to the file OUTPUT, and starts a new OUTPUTLINE. GRABINPUTLINE will be the name of the procedure that picks up and continues the processing of the input line after the initial character or initial word is dealt with. GRABWORD will be the name of the procedure that tries to read the word starting with the character previously read. This suggests that it needs to take that character as an argument – GRABWORD(CHAR1 : CHAR). Finally, INSERTWORD will be the procedure that inserts the appropriate part of WORD (as determined by WORDINDEX) into the array OUTPUTLINE. Given these decisions, we may present a complete outline of PROCESSINPUTLINE as in Figure 10-11.

Figure 10-11. First Outline of PROCESSINPUTLINE.

```
procedure PROCESSINPUTLINE;
    var
        NEXTCHARACTER : CHAR;
        WORD          : array[1..COMMENTWIDTH] of CHAR;
        WORDINDEX     : 1..COMMENTWIDTH;

    procedure SHIPOUTPUTLINE;
    begin
        Body of the procedure
    end; (* SHIPOUTPUTLINE *)

    procedure PRINTBLANKLINE;
    begin
        Body of the procedure
    end; (* PRINTBLANKLINE *)

    procedure GRABWORD(CHAR1 : CHAR);
    begin
        Body of the procedure
    end; (* GRABWORD *)

    procedure INSERTWORD;
    begin
        Body of the procedure
    end;  (* INSERTWORD *)
```

Figure 10-11. Continued.

```
procedure GRABINPUTLINE;
begin
   Body of the procedure
end;  (* GRABINPUTLINE *)

begin (* Main Program *)
   if Input line is blank then
      begin
         SHIPOUTPUTLINE;
         PRINTBLANKLINE;
         READLN(INPUT)
      end
   else
   begin
      READ(INPUT,NEXTCHARACTER);
      if ((NEXTCHARACTER = SPACE) and not(STARTING)) then
         begin
            SHIPOUTPUTLINE.
            OUTPUTLINE[4] := NEXTCHARACTER;
            LINEINDEX     := 5;
            GRABINPUTLINE
         end
      else
         begin
            GRABWORD(NEXTCHARACTER);
            if Word doesn't fit in OUTPUTLINE then
               SHIPOUTPUTLINE;
            INSERTWORD;
            if DONE then
               SHIPOUTPUTLINE
            else
               GRABINPUTLINE
         end
   end
end (* PROCESS INPUTLINE *)
```

Next consider the manipulation of WORDs. Both NEXTWORD and GRABWORD will use WORDINDEX in the same manner that LINEINDEX is used. Namely, WORDINDEX will always indicate the first unused position in WORD. Then INSERTWORD can be outlined as follows:

```
procedure INSERTWORD;
begin
    if (The last entry in OUTPUTLINE is not SPACE
    and
       The first entry in WORD is not SPACE)   then
       Add a SPACE to OUTPUTLINE;
    Copy the entries from 1 to WORDINDEX-1 in WORD over
       to the corresponding points in OUTPUTLINE;
    Increment LINEINDEX appropriately
end;   (* INSERTWORD *)
```

This is now easy to refine, as seen in Program 10-1.

To decide whether or not the WORD read will fit in OUTPUTLINE, we must decide whether the number of characters in the WORD is less than or equal to the number of available positions in OUTPUTLINE. The number of characters in WORD is simply WORDINDEX-1 (since WORDINDEX always points to the first unused position). The number of available spaces in OUTPUTLINE is simply

```
(COMMENTWIDTH - 2) - (LINEINDEX - 1)
```

or

```
COMMENTWIDTH - LINEINDEX - 1
```

Thus, if

```
WORDINDEX > COMMENTWIDTH - LINEINDEX
```

the WORD will not fit in the remainder of the present OUTPUTLINE.

Finally, consider the condition defining a blank line. By definition, a blank line is one with no characters. Thus it must be that: when supposedly at the beginning of a blank line, the predicate EOLN(INPUT) will be true. (That is, the file will contain two successive end-of-line markers.) With these considerations, we may produce our first refinement of PROCESSINPUTLINE, as shown in Figure 10-12.

Figure 10-12.   First Refinement of PROCESSINPUTLINE.

```
procedure PROCESSINPUTLINE;
  var
    NEXTCHARACTER : CHAR;
    WORD          : array[1..COMMENTWIDTH] of CHAR;
    WORDINDEX     : 1..COMMENTWIDTH;
  procedure SHIPOUTPUTLINE;
    var
        COUNTER : 1..COMMENTWIDTH;
  begin
    for COUNTER := LINEINDEX to COMMENTWIDTH-2 do
       OUTPUTLINE[COUNTER] := SPACE;
    for COUNTER := 1 to COMMENTWIDTH do
       WRITE(OUTPUT,OUTPUTLINE[COUNTER]);
    WRITELN(OUTPUT);
    STARTOUTPUTLINE;
    LINEINDEX := 4
  end; (* SHIPOUTPUTLINE *)
  procedure PRINTBLANKLINE;
    var
        COUNTER : 1..COMMENTWIDTH;
  begin
    WRITE(OUTPUT,SPACE,ASTERISK);
    for COUNTER := 3 to COMMENTWIDTH-1 do
       WRITE(OUTPUT,SPACE);
    WRITELN(OUTPUT,ASTERISK)
  end; (* PRINTBLANKLINE *)
  procedure GRABWORD(CHAR1 : CHAR);
  begin
    Body of the procedure
  end; (* GRABWORD *)
  procedure INSERTWORD;
    var
        COUNTER : 1..COMMENTWIDTH;
  begin
    if ((OUTPUTLINE[LINEINDEX-1] <> SPACE)
        and
        (WORD[1] <> SPACE))   then
        begin
           OUTPUTLINE[LINEINDEX] := SPACE;
           LINEINDEX := LINEINDEX + 1
        end;
    for COUNTER := 1 to WORDINDEX - 1 do
       OUTPUTLINE[LINEINDEX + COUNTER - 1] := WORD[COUNTER];
    LINEINDEX := LINEINDEX + WORDINDEX - 1
  end; (* INSERTWORD *)
```

Figure 10-12. Continued.

```
procedure GRABINPUTLINE;
begin
    Body of the procedure
end;  (* GRABINPUTLINE *)

begin (* Main Program *)
    if EOLN(INPUT) then
        begin
            SHIPOUTPUTLINE;
            PRINTBLANKLINE;
            READLN(INPUT)
        end
    else
    begin
        READ(INPUT,NEXTCHARACTER);
        if ((NEXTCHARACTER = SPACE) and not(STARTING)) then
            begin
                SHIPOUTPUTLINE;
                OUTPUTLINE[4] := NEXTCHARACTER;
                LINEINDEX    := 5;
                GRABINPUTLINE
            end
        else
            begin
                GRABWORD(NEXTCHARACTER);
                if WORDINDEX > COMMENTWIDTH - LINEINDEX then
                    SHIPOUTPUTLINE;
                INSERTWORD;
                if DONE then
                    SHIPOUTPUTLINE
                else
                    GRABINPUTLINE
            end
    end
end (*PROCESS INPUTLINE *)
```

Now it remains for us to develop the procedures GRABWORD and GRABINPUTLINE. To begin with GRABWORD, you will recall that it takes an argument CHAR1. This is to be the first character of the WORD it is trying to read. Thus we may outline GRABWORD as follows:

```
procedure GRABWORD(CHAR1 : CHAR);
begin
    WORD[1] := CHAR1;
    WORDINDEX := 2;
    while ((WORD[WORDINDEX-1]<>SPACE) and not(EOLN(INPUT))
            and The end of the comment has not been reached) do
    begin
        Read the next character into NEXTCHARACTER and also
                into WORD[WORDINDEX];
        Increment WORDINDEX
    end; (* while *)

    if The end of the comment has been reached then
        begin
            DONE := TRUE;
            Other housekeeping
        end
end;  (* GRABWORD *)
```

How do we know when the end of the input comment is reached? It occurs when the character just read is an asterisk and the INPUT file window is looking at a right parenthesis. Thus, if we guarantee that the last character read from INPUT is always present in NEXTCHARACTER, we can define a Boolean function ENDOFCOMMENT to recognize this:

```
function ENDOFCOMMENT : BOOLEAN;
begin
    ENDOFCOMMENT :=
        ((NEXTCHARACTER = ASTERISK) and (INPUT^ = RIGHTPAREN))
end; (* ENDOFCOMMENT *)
```

Thus we may refine GRABWORD to its final form, as seen in Program 10-1.

The last bit of "housekeeping" appearing when ENDOFCOMMENT is TRUE is required for the following reasons. The last cycle through the while loop preceding this conditional will have put an asterisk into WORD at the end of the word being read in. Decrementing WORDINDEX has the effect of dropping this asterisk from the end of the word. The last READLN is included to move the INPUT file window just past the closing right parenthesis of the comment symbol "*)".

Finally, we must tackle the procedure GRABINPUTLINE. Given the structure of the program we have developed thus far, this procedure can expect to be called when at least one character or word has been read from the input line and inserted into the OUTPUTLINE. The task of GRABINPUTLINE is to continue the processing of the input line until the end of that line is reached, the end of the comment is reached, or (just possibly) the end of the file is reached. In very rough outline, it must repeatedly do the following: after reading a character, it must examine that character and make a decision:

1. If the character is an asterisk and the end of the comment has been reached, it must call SHIPOUTPUTLINE and do some other "housekeeping."

2. If the character is a SPACE then it has several cases to deal with, depending on the value of LINEINDEX. We will examine these later.

3. If the character is not a SPACE, then it must be the beginning of a word. This word should be read into WORD and inserted into OUTPUTLINE, of course worrying about whether it will fit and acting accordingly.

Consider the situation in which the character that has been read is a SPACE. If 4 < LINEINDEX < COMMENTWIDTH-1, we will simply treat it as a single unit word and transfer it directly to OUTPUTLINE at position LINEINDEX. Our concern, however, is not to add unnecessary spaces at the beginning of an OUTPUTLINE. In fact, the only SPACE that should be entered at the beginning of an OUTPUTLINE should come from the beginning of an input line. Since GRABINPUTLINE never gets to deal with the first character of the input line, it should never try to insert a space at the beginning of OUTPUTLINE. Thus if it has read a SPACE as the character, and if LINEINDEX = 4, it should simply ignore this space by doing nothing at all in this cycle. And if LINEINDEX >= COMMENTWIDTH-1, not only should the SPACE be ignored, but a new OUTPUTLINE should be started.

Finally, if the character read is not a SPACE, we can detail the work as follows:

1. Obtain the word starting with the character just read.

2. If the word will not fit in the current OUTPUTLINE, call SHIPOUTPUTLINE to terminate the present line, send it to the file OUTPUT, and start a new OUTPUTLINE.

3. Insert the word in OUTPUTLINE.

4. Check whether DONE has become TRUE. (This might come about from the action of reading the word.) If so, call SHIPOUTPUTLINE.

What are the conditions under which GRABINPUTLINE should continue repeating its actions? Certainly, it must stop if it reaches the end of the INPUT file, if it reaches the end of the INPUT line, and if the end of the input comment has been reached. Under all other conditions, there are more characters to be read from the current input comment line, and the procedure should continue.

Collecting these observations,we may design GRABOUTPUTLINE as shown in Program 10-1. We have now concluded our development of procedures and functions.

Our systematic approach has enabled us to break down the problem into manageable pieces, each of which has been built. By being clear and precise about the overall program requirements and by using the same methodology for the component parts, we have been able to design and construct the requisite program (Program 10-1). Note that the comment box was, in fact, processed by the program itself.

Program 10-1. The Complete Program COMMENT.

```
program COMMENT(INPUT,OUTPUT);
(*  ------------------------------------------------------------  *
 *       This program transforms ordinary comments in Pascal     *
 *    programs into boxed comments, filling the lines in the box  *
 *    where appropriate. It only transforms those comments whose  *
 *    opening symbol is at the far left side of the line on which *
 *    they begin. It leaves all other comments, and the program   *
 *    proper, untouched. It also attempts to preserve the         *
 *    indenting and blank line structure of the original comment. *
 *       The input is the original source program.                *
 *       The output is the transformed program.                   *
 *       The principal procedure is BOXCOMMENT. This procedure    *
 *    expects to be called when the INPUT file window is          *
 *    positioned at the second character of a comment that must   *
 *    be boxed. It reads through this entire comment,             *
 *    outputtingthe properly boxed form to the file OUTPUT.       *
 *    When the procedure finishes running, the INPUT file         *
 *    window is positioned after the close of the comment just    *
 *    processed.                                                   *
 *  ------------------------------------------------------------  *)
```

Program 10-1. Continued.

```
const
    LEFTPAREN    = '(';
    RIGHTPAREN   = ')';
    ASTERISK     = '*';
    HYPHEN       = '-';
    SPACE        = ' ';
    TABSYM       = '    ';
    COMMENTOPEN  = '(*';
    COMMENTCLOSE = '*)';
    COMMENTWIDTH = 60;

function COMMENTSTART : BOOLEAN;
    var
        FIRSTCHAR : CHAR;
begin
    READ(INPUT,FIRSTCHAR);
    if ((FIRSTCHAR = LEFTPAREN) and (INPUT^ = ASTERISK)) then
        begin
            COMMENTSTART := TRUE;
            READ(INPUT,FIRSTCHAR)
        end
    else
        begin
            COMMENTSTART := FALSE;
            WRITE(OUTPUT,FIRSTCHAR);
        end
end; (* COMMENTSTART *)

procedure TRANSFER;
    var LETTER : CHAR;
begin
    while (not(EOF(INPUT)) and not(EOLN(INPUT))) do
    begin
        READ(INPUT,LETTER);
        WRITE(OUTPUT,LETTER);
    end;
    if not(EOF(INPUT)) then
        READLN(INPUT);
    WRITELN(OUTPUT)
end; (* TRANSFER *)
```

Program 10-1.   Continued.

```
procedure BOXCOMMENT;
   var
      DONE,STARTING  :  BOOLEAN;
      LINEINDEX      :  1..COMMENTWIDTH;
      OUTPUTLINE     :  array[1..COMMENTWIDTH] of CHAR;

   procedure STARTOUTPUTLINE;
   begin
      OUTPUTLINE[1]   := SPACE.
      OUTPUTLINE[2]   := ASTERISK;
      OUTPUTLINE[3]   := SPACE;

      OUTPUTLINE[COMMENTWIDTH-1] := SPACE;
      OUTPUTLINE[COMMENTWIDTH]   := ASTERISK;
   end; (* STARTOUTPUTLINE *)

   procedure PRINTTOPLINE;
      var
         COUNTER : 1..COMMENTWIDTH;
   begin
      WRITE(OUTPUT,LEFTPAREN);
      WRITE(OUTPUT,ASTERISK);
      for COUNTER := 1 to COMMENTWIDTH - 3 do
         WRITE(OUTPUT,HYPHEN);
      WRITE(OUTPUT,ASTERISK);
      WRITELN(OUTPUT)
   end; (* PRINTTOPLINE *)

   procedure PRINTBOTTOMLINE;
      var
         COUNTER : 1..COMMENTWIDTH;
   begin
      WRITE(OUTPUT,SPACE);
      WRITE(OUTPUT,ASTERISK);
      for COUNTER := 1 to COMMENTWIDTH - 3 do
         WRITE(OUTPUT,HYPHEN);
      WRITE(OUTPUT,ASTERISK);
      WRITE(OUTPUT,RIGHTPAREN);
      WRITELN(OUTPUT)
   end; (* PRINTBOTTOMLINE *)
```

Program 10-1. Continued.

```
procedure PROCESSINPUTLINE;
   var
      NEXTCHARACTER : CHAR;
      WORD : array[1..COMMENTWIDTH] of CHAR;
      WORDINDEX : 1..COMMENTWIDTH;

   procedure SHIPOUTPUTLINE;
      var
         COUNTER : 1..COMMENTWIDTH;
   begin
      for COUNTER := LINEINDEX to COMMENTWIDTH - 2 do
         OUTPUTLINE[COUNTER] := SPACE;
      for COUNTER := 1 TO COMMENTWIDTH do
         WRITE(OUTPUT,OUTPUTLINE[COUNTER]);
      WRITELN(OUTPUT);
      LINEINDEX := 4;
      STARTOUTPUTLINE
   end; (* SHIPOUTPUTLINE *)


   function ENDOFCOMMENT : BOOLEAN;
   begin
      ENDOFCOMMENT :=
         ((NEXTCHARACTER = ASTERISK) and
         (INPUT^ = RIGHTPAREN    ))
   end; (* ENDOFCOMMENT *)


   procedure PRINTBLANKLINE;
      var
         COUNTER : 1..COMMENTWIDTH;
   begin
      WRITE(OUTPUT,SPACE);
      WRITE(OUTPUT,ASTERISK);
      for COUNTER := 3 to COMMENTWIDTH-1 do
         WRITE(OUTPUT,SPACE);
      WRITE(OUTPUT,ASTERISK);
      WRITELN(OUTPUT)
   end; (* PRINTBLANKLINE *)
```

Program 10-1. Continued.

```
procedure GRABWORD(CHAR1 : CHAR);
begin
  WORD[1] := CHAR1;
  WORDINDEX := 2;
while ((WORD[WORDINDEX-1]<>SPACE) and not(EOLN(INPUT))
      and not(ENDOFCOMMENT)) do
    begin
      READ(INPUT, NEXTCHARACTER);
      WORD[WORDINDEX] := NEXTCHARACTER;
      WORDINDEX := WORDINDEX + 1
    end;
    if ENDOFCOMMENT then
      begin
        DONE := TRUE;
        WORDINDEX := WORDINDEX - 1;
        READ(INPUT,NEXTCHARACTER)
      end
end; (* GRABWORD *)


procedure INSERTWORD;
  var COUNTER : 1..COMMENTWIDTH;
begin
if OUTPUTLINE[LINEINDEX-1] <> SPACE then
    begin
      OUTPUTLINE[LINEINDEX] := SPACE;
      LINEINDEX := LINEINDEX + 1
    end;
  for COUNTER := 1 TO WORDINDEX-1 do
    OUTPUTLINE[LINEINDEX + COUNTER - 1]
                  := WORD[COUNTER];
  LINEINDEX := LINEINDEX + WORDINDEX - 1;
end; (* INSERTWORD *)
```

Program 10-1. Continued.

```
procedure GRABINPUTLINE;

    function READINGOK : BOOLEAN;
    begin
        READINGOK :=
            (not(DONE) and not(EOF(INPUT))
                        and not(EOLN(INPUT)))
    end; (* READINGOK *)

begin
    while READINGOK do
    begin
        READ(INPUT,NEXTCHARACTER);
        if ENDOFCOMMENT then
            begin
                SHIPOUTPUTLINE;
                DONE := TRUE;
                READ(INPUT,NEXTCHARACTER)
            end
        else if NEXTCHARACTER = SPACE then
            begin
                if ((4 < LINEINDEX)
                and (LINEINDEX < COMMENTWIDTH-1)) then
                    begin
                        OUTPUTLINE[LINEINDEX] := NEXTCHARACTER;
                        LINEINDEX := LINEINDEX + 1
                    end
                else if (LINEINDEX >= COMMENTWIDTH-1) then
                    SHIPOUTPUTLINE
            end
        else
            begin
                GRABWORD(NEXTCHARACTER);
                if WORDINDEX > COMMENTWIDTH-LINEINDEX then
                    SHIPOUTPUTLINE;
                INSERTWORD;
                if DONE then
                    SHIPOUTPUTLINE;
            end
    end
end; (* GRABINPUTLINE *)
```

Program 10-1. Continued.

```
begin (* PROCESSINPUTLINE *)
     if EOLN(INPUT) then
     begin
       SHIPOUTPUTLINE;
       PRINTBLANKLINE;
       READLN(INPUT)
     end
   else
   begin
     READ(INPUT,NEXTCHARACTER);
     if ((NEXTCHARACTER = SPACE) and not(STARTING)) then
       begin
         SHIPOUTPUTLINE;
         OUTPUTLINE[4] := NEXTCHARACTER;
         LINEINDEX    := 5;
         GRABINPUTLINE;
       end
     else
       begin
         GRABWORD(NEXTCHARACTER);
         if WORDINDEX > COMMENTWIDTH-LINEINDEX then
           SHIPOUTPUTLINE;
         INSERTWORD;
         if DONE then
           SHIPOUTPUTLINE
         else
           GRABINPUTLINE
       end (* else *)
     end (* else *)
end; (* PROCESSINPUTLINE *)
```

Program 10-1. Continued.

```
begin  (* BOXCOMMENT *)
    DONE := FALSE;
    STARTOUTPUTLINE;
    LINEINDEX := 4;
    PRINTTOPLINE;

    STARTING := TRUE;
    PROCESSINPUTLINE;
    if not(DONE) then
        READLN(INPUT);
    STARTING := FALSE;

    while not(DONE) do
    begin
        PROCESSINPUTLINE;
        if not(DONE) then
            READLN(INPUT)
    end;

    PRINTBOTTOMLINE;
end; (* BOXCOMMENT *)

begin  (* Main Program *)
    while not(EOF(INPUT)) do
        if COMMENTSTART then
            BOXCOMMENT
        else
            TRANSFER
end.
```

Exercises

Exercise 10-1   An adjacency matrix is an nxn matrix M all of whose entries are either 0 or 1. Such matrices can be used by anthropologists to study family relationships in villages: 1 entered in M[i,j] means that i and j are known to be related, while 0 indicates that they are not known to be related. Obviously, we will always have M[i,j] = M[j,i] in this case. Since M is nxn, we can construct the products

   M*M, M*M*M, . . .

which we will denote by M**2, M**3, . . ., and so forth (see Exercise 7-8). It is possible to prove the following:

   a) There is a k such that M**k = M**k+1;
   b) If L = M**k, then i and j belong to the same family if and only if L[i,j] = 1.

   Construct a program RELATIVES that takes two files, NAMES and RELS as input. The file NAMES is simply a sequence of STRINGs that are names of people: the ith entry in NAMES is the name of the ith person. RELS is an adjacency matrix containing information an anthropologist might be able to discover. The program should read RELS into a matrix M and then compute the matrix L = M**k, as previously described. The program should then use L and the file NAMES to print out the family groups on the terminal.

Exercise 10-2   The "game" of LIFE was invented by the English mathematician John Conway. It is played on an m x n grid. Each cell of the grid is capable of being empty or holding a single life form. Each cell is thought of as having up to 8 neighboring cells: those immediately adjacent to it horizontally and vertically and those adjacent to it along diagonals. Obviously, cells at the edges or corners have fewer neighbors. The "game" starts with a given placement of organisms in cells. New generations of organisms are produced according to the following rules:

   1. An organism in cell C survives to the next generation if the number of occupied neighbor cells of C in the present generation is either 2 or 3; otherwise, it dies and C becomes unoccupied in the next generation.

2. An organism is born in an empty cell C at the next generation if the number of occupied neighbor cells of C in the present generation is exactly C.

Write a program LIFE that will accept as input a file containing an initial placement of organisms in cells. The program should compute the successive generations according to rules 1 and 2 and print a copy of each generation on the terminal. [Note that the rules for the transition from one generation to the next must be applied simultaneously to all the cells in the grid. Thus, presumably, the program will need to work with two grids: one for the present generation and one for the next generation.]

Exercise 10-3 Given a page size PAGELENGTH lines long by PAGEWIDTH characters wide, a piece of text is regarded as being properly formatted on the page provided the following are all satisfied:

1. A page number occurs in the upper right-hand corner.
2. A blank line follows the line containing the page number.
3. Paragraphs are indented five spaces.
4. Each line (except the last lines of paragraphs) is filled in the sense that the next word in the current sentence would not fit on the given line within the PAGEWIDTH limit.
5. Each line (except the last lines of paragraphs) is justified in the sense that the last character of the last word on the line occurs exactly at the right-hand margin – that is, exactly PAGEWIDTH characters across from the left-hand margin. (This is achieved by adding extra blanks between words as is necessary to push the last word over to the right. These blanks should be distributed as evenly as possible between all the words on the line.)
6. There are at most PAGELENGTH lines on the page including the page number line and the following blank line.

Write a program FORMAT that accepts a file TEXT of English text as input and produces a file FORMATTEDTEXT as output. The output text should be formatted according to the foregoing rules. In addition, any line of the input text that begins with a blank should signal the start of a new paragraph.

Exercise 10-4 Write a program BLACKJACK that plays the dealer in the game of Blackjack against the user at the terminal. (See Exercise 9-4). The rules run as follows:

1. The dealer deals one card face down to the player and one card face down to herself.

2. The player makes a bet.

3. The player may request hits (additional cards) one at a time from the dealer. This continues until the player stands pat (wants no more cards) or the total score of the player's cards exceeds 21.

4. If the player is standing pat, the dealer takes additional cards until either her score exceeds 16, at which time she must stand pat, or her score exceeds 21.

5. If both player and dealer have scores less than 21 (and the dealer's score is at least 16), the winner is the one with the highest score. Ties go to the dealer.

6. If the player receives a natural 21 (an ace with a facecard or ten), he wins immediately, unless the dealer also has a natural.

Your program should be decently interactive, with the dealer giving the appropriate information to the player at the appropriate time. It should also keep a running tab of the player's wins and losses and report this when the player stops playing.

Exercise 10-5   A concordance for a piece of text is a list of all the words that occur in the text together with a count of the number of times that they occur. Write a program CONCORDANCE that takes a file TEXT as input and outputs a concordance for TEXT on the terminal. You may assume the following about TEXT:

1. There is a maximum number of MAXNUMWORDS of distinct words that occur in TEXT.

2. There is a maximum length MAXWORDLENGTH of words occurring in TEXT.

For the first version of your program, the output concordance should be in the order in which the words are first encountered in the text. When this version is completed and debugged, revise and extend it so that the concordance is output in alphabetical order. Then prepare a third version that outputs the concordance in ascending frequency of occurrence of the words, and within groups of words with the same frequency of occurrence list the words in alphabetical order.

Appendix A

Pascal at a Glance

We present below a compressed description of the syntax of Pascal by means of informal diagrams and skeletons. This is intended as a quick summary, and does not describe all the semantic restrictions for the code to be correct. Consult the appropriate chapter for full details. When there are alternate forms of a given kind of syntactic entity (e.g., statement), the various alternatives are listed below the appropriate heading, with the alternatives separated by blank lines.

program

```
program identifier ( identifier_list );
block .
```

block

```
const
   identifier = constant;

type
   identifier = type;

var
   identifier_list : type;

function/procedure declarations

begin
   statements
end
```

procedure declaration

```
procedure identifier ( parameter_list );
block;
```

function declaration

> function *identifier* (*parameter__list*) : *type__identifier*
> *block;*

parameter__list

> *parameter__declaration;*

parameter__declaration

> *identifier list* : *identifier*
>
> var *identifier__list* : *identifier*

statements

> *statement;*

statement

> *variable* := *expression*
>
> *function identifier* := *expression*
>
> *procedure__identifier* (*expression__list*)
>
> begin
>   *statements*
> end
>
> if *expression* then
>   *statement*
> else
>   *statement*
>
> case *expression* of
>   *constant__list* : *statement;*
> end
>
> while *expression* do
>   *statement*
>
> repeat
>   *statements*
> until
>   *expression*
>
>   downto
> for *identifier* := *expression* to   *expression* do
>   *statement*

expression

    simple__expression

$$\begin{array}{c}\blacklozenge\\<\\>\end{array}$$

simple__expression   <>   *simple__expression*

$$\begin{array}{c}>=\\<=\\\text{in}\end{array}$$

simple__expression

+		+		+		+	
-	*inter*	-	*inter*	-	...	-	*inter*
or		or		or		or	

term

	*			*			*	
	/			/			/	
factor	div	*factor*	div	...	div	*factor*
	mod		mod		mod	
	and		and		and	

factor

    unsigned constant

    variable

    function__identifier (*expression__list*)

    (*expression*)

    not *factor*

    [*expression__list*]

variable

    identifier

    variable [*expression__list*]

    variable . *identifier*

    identifier

type

>   *simple__type*
>
>   {packed} array[*simple__type__list*] of *type*
>
>   file of *type*
>
>   record
>   *field__list*
>   end

field__list

>   *identifier__list* : *type*;

simple__type__list

>   *simple__type*,

simple__type

>   *identifier*
>
>   (*identifier__list*)
>
>   *constant..constant*

constant

>   +
>   – *identifier*
>
>   +
>   – *unsigned__number*
>
>   '*character*'

unsigned constant

>   *identifier*
>
>   *unsigned number*
>
>   nil
>
>   '*character__sequence*'

identifier__list

>   *identifier*,

identifier

>   *letter alpha-digit__sequence*

alpha-digit__sequence

>   *alpha-digit*

alpha-digit

> *letter*

> *digit*

letter

A B C D E F G H I J K L M N O P Q R S T U V W X Y Z

a b c d e f g h i j k l m n o p q r s t u v w x y z

digit

0 1 2 3 4 5 6 7 8 9

unsigned number

> *digit__sequence*

> *digit__sequence.digit__sequence*

> *digit__sequence* E *digit__sequence*
> $\begin{array}{c}+\\-\end{array}$

digit__sequence

> *digit*

character__sequence

> *character*

character

> *letter*

> *digit*

> *other__characters*

other__characters

Appendix B

Reserved Words for Pascal

The 35 reserved words of Pascal are as follows:

and	end	nil	set
array	file	not	then
begin	for	of	to
case	function	or	type
const	goto	packed	until
div	if	procedure	var
do	in	program	while
downto	label	record	with
else	mod	repeat	

The special symbols for Pascal are the following:

±	:	(	)
–	,	=	]
*	;	{	}
/	<	<	>
<>	.	<=	>=
|	..	(*	*)

Appendix C

Intrinsic Functions and Procedures

The standard functions and procedures listed below are assumed to be predeclared in every implementation of Pascal. Because of this, they may be redeclared in any program as necessary. Of course, various implementations may predeclare other procedures and functions. Note also that many implementations extend the capabilities of some of these standard objects (for example, extending READ and WRITE to allow input-output of enumeration types.)

STANDARD FUNCTIONS

Arithmetic Functions

ABS(X)   — computes the absolute value of X, where the type of X must be either real or integer. The type of the result is the same as the type of X.

SQR(X)   — computes the square of X, where the type of X must be either real or integer. The type of the result is the same as the type of X.

In each of the following, the type of X may be real or integer, and the type of the result is real.

SIN(X)   — the trigonometric sine of X.
COS(X)   — the trigonometric cosine of X.
EXP(X)   — the constant e raised to the power X.
LN(X)   — the natural logarithm of X.
SQRT(X)   — the square root of X.
ARCTAN(X)   — the trigonometric inverse of TAN(X).

Boolean Functions (Predicates)

ODD(X)   — the type of X must be integer; returns TRUE if X is an odd integer, and returns FALSE if X is even or zero.

EOF(F)   — returns TRUE if the file F has reached the end-of-file status, and returns FALSE otherwise.

EOLN(F)   — returns TRUE if the textfile F has reached the end-of-line status, and returns FALSE otherwise.

Transfer functions

TRUNC(X)   — X must be real; returns the truncation of X to its integral part.

ROUND(X)   — X must be real; returns the result of rounding X to the nearest integer.

ORD(X)   — X must be of some scalar type (including possibly type CHAR and type Boolean); the result is of type integer, and is the ordinal number of X in the enumerated set consisting of the type of which X is a member.

CHR(X)   — X must of type integer; the result is of type CHAR, and is the character whose ordinal number in the enumeration of CHAR is X (if it exists).

Miscellaneous Standard Functions

SUCC(X)   — X must belong to a scalar or subrange type and must not be the last element of that type in its standard enumeration; the result is the successor to X in that type.

PRED(X)   — X must belong to a scalar or subrange type and must not be the first element of that type in its standard enumeration; the result is the predecessor of X in that type.

STANDARD PROCEDURES

Input and Output Procedures

READ(F,V)

— F must be a textfile. If V is of type CHAR, this causes one character to be input from the file F and stored in the variable V. If V is a variable of type integer or real, the system attempts to read a sequence of characters making up such a number from the file F. Leading blanks and end of line characters should be skipped over. The sequence of characters making up the number is terminated by any character which cannot be part of a numeric expression of that type. The expression READ(F,V1, . . .,Vk) is equivalent to

    begin READ(F,V1); . . ., READ(F,Vk) end.

Finally, READ(V1, . . .,Vk) is equivalent to

    READ(INPUT,V1, . . .,Vk).

READLN(F,V)

— equivalent to

    begin READ(F,V); READLN(F) end,

where READLN(F) causes the file window F^ to be positioned at the beginning of the next line, skipping the remainder of the current line of F. READLN (F,V1, . . .,Vk) is equivalent to

    begin READ(F,V1, . . .,Vk); READLN(F) end,

and READLN(V1, . . .,Vk) is equivalent to

    READLN(INPUT,V1, . . .,Vk).

WRITE(F,P)

— F must be a textfile and P is an expression of one of the forms E, E:M, or E:M:N, where M and N are integers. First, WRITE(F,P1, . . .,Pk) is equivalent to

    begin WRITE(F,P1; . . .WRITE(F,Pk) end,

and WRITE(P1, . . .,Pk) is equivalent to

    WRITE(OUTPUT,P1, . . .,Pk).

In general, the expression E represents a value to be written onto the file F, and may be of type CHAR, STRING, integer, real, or Boolean. If the representation of E requires less than M columns to write, then enough leading blanks are written so that the entire representation occupies exactly M columns. If M is omitted (i.e., if P is E), then an implementation-dependent default value of M is used. The form E:M:N is used only when E is of type real.

If E is of type CHAR or STRING, the appropriate written version of E is written on F, with leading blanks as determined by M.

If E is of type integer, the decimal representation of E is written on F with leading blanks as determined by M.

If E is of type real and P is E:M:N, a fixed-point decimal representation of E is written on F with N digits to the right of the decimal point, and leading blanks as determined by M. Note that the decimal point must be counted in determining the number of leading blanks to print. If P is E:M and E is of type real, a floating-point representation of E is written on F with leading blanks determined by M.

If E is of type Boolean, the appropriate word TRUE or FALSE is written on F with leading blanks as determined by M.

WRITELN(F,P) — is equivalent to

```
begin WRITE(F,P); WRITE(F) end
```

where WRITELN(F) causes a new line to be started on F. The expression WRITELN(F,P1, . . . ,Pk) is equivalent to

```
begin WRITE(F,P1, . . . ,Pk); WRITELN(F) end
```

and the expression WRITELN(P1, . . .,Pk) is equivalent to

```
WRITELN(OUTPUT,P1, . . . ,Pk)
```

PAGE(F) — F must be a textfile; causes a skip to the start of a new page of F when F is printed.

File Handling Procedures

PUT(F) — causes the value of the file buffer variable F^ to be appended to the end of the file F. This procedure operates successfully only if just prior to its being called, the function EOF(F) would have returned TRUE. Then after execution of PUT(F), EOF(F) remains true, and the value of F^ becomes undefined.

GET(F)   —causes the "read/write" head to be advanced to the next component of the file F and assigns this component of the file window variable F^. If no next component exists, then EOF(F) becomes TRUE and the value of F^ becomes undefined. GET(F) successfully operates only if just prior to its execution, the function EOF(F) would have returned FALSE.

RESET(F)   — causes the "read/write" head to be repositioned at the beginning of the file F and assigns the first component of F to the file window variable F^ as its value, provided that F is a non-empty file. If F is in fact empty, EOF(F) becomes false and the value of F is undefined. [Note that various implementations may allow extra parameters to allow the connection of F with external (disk) files.]

REWRITE(F)   — causes the current value associated with F to be discarded and a new output file started. EOF(F) becomes TRUE. [NOTE that various implementations may allow extra parameters to permit the connection of F with external (disk) files.]

Appendix D

Character Code Tables

Included below are the tables of the major coding schemes for the ordinal numbers corresponding to the entities of type CHAR. In each case, ♭ indicates the blank character, and missing numbers correspond to non-printing "control characters" which are not part of the type CHAR.

EBCDIC Codes

64	≠	110	>	146	k	195	C	228	U
70	¢	111	?	147	l	196	D	229	V
72	<	122	:	148	m	197	E	230	W
73	(	123	°	149	n	198	F	231	X
74	+	124	@	150	o	199	G	232	Y
75	|	126	'	151	p	200	H	233	Z
80	&	127	=	152	q	201	I	240	0
90	!	128	"	153	r	209	J	241	1
91	$	129	a	162	s	210	K	242	2
92	*	130	b	163	t	211	L	243	3
93	)	131	c	164	u	212	M	244	4
94	;	132	d	165	v	213	N	245	5
95	-	133	e	166	w	214	O	246	6
96	-	134	f	167	x	215	P	247	7
97	/	135	g	168	y	216	Q	248	8
107	,	136	h	169	z	217	R	249	9
108	%	137	i	193	A	226	S		
109	_	145	j	194	B	227	T		

ASCII Codes

32	≠	64	@	96	'		
33	!	65	A	97	a		
34	''	66	B	98	b		
35	#	67	C	99	c		
36	$	68	D	100	d		
37	%	69	E	101	e		
38	&	70	F	102	f		
39	,	71	G	103	g		
40	(	72	H	104	h		
41	)	73	I	105	i		
42	*	74	J	106	j		
43	+	75	K	107	k		
44	'	76	L	108	l		
45	−	77	M	109	m		
46	.	78	N	110	n		
47	/	79	O	111	o		
48	0	80	P	112	p		
49	1	81	Q	113	q		
50	2	82	R	114	r		
51	3	83	S	115	s		
52	4	84	T	116	t		
53	5	85	U	117	u		
54	6	86	V	118	v		
55	7	87	W	119	w		
56	8	88	X	120	x		
57	9	89	Y	121	y		
58	:	90	Z	122	z		
59	;	91	[	123	{		
60	<	92	/	124			
61	=	93	]	125	}		
62	>	94	___				
63	?	95	⊥				

CDC Scientific Character Set with 64 Elements

0	:	16	P	32	5	48	=
1	A	17	Q	33	6	49	[
2	B	18	R	34	7	50	]
3	C	19	S	35	8	51	%
4	D	20	T	36	9	52	≠
5	E	21	U	37	+	53	
6	F	22	V	38	−	54	
7	G	23	W	39	*	55	
8	H	24	X	40	/	56	
9	I	25	Y	41	(	57	
10	J	26	Z	42	)	58	<
11	K	27	0	43	$	59	>
12	L	28	1	44	=	60	<
13	M	29	2	45	≠	61	>
14	N	30	3	46	,	62	−
15	O	31	4	47	.	63	;

Appendix E

UCSD Pascal

One of the most popular implementations of Pascal is the UCSD Pascal system developed at the University of California at San Diego. It is widely available, in particular, on Apple computers and Digital Equipment PDP-11 computers. This appendix describes the few important differences between UCSD Pascal and standard Pascal as we have described it in the text.

Program Headings

The UCSD Pascal compiler ignores the list of file identifiers following the program identifier in the program heading. The compiler automatically opens the three files INPUT, OUTPUT, and KEYBOARD, all of type INTERACTIVE (see below). Any other files to be opened must be declared as variables in the program's VAR section, and the file identifier connected with the external file name by use of a RESET or REWRITE command.

Strings

The UCSD Pascal system provides a predeclared type STRING. Variables of this type are essentially PACKED ARRAYS of CHAR, but may vary in length dynamically. The length of a STRING variable is obtained using the intrinsic function LENGTH. The default maximum length of a STRING variable is 80 characters, but may be changed by appending the desired maximum length in [ ] following the identifier STRING in the variable declaration, as in the example below:

```
VAR
   TITLE : STRING;       (* Defaults to maximum length 80 *)

   NAME  : STRING[20];   (* Restricts NAME to strings of
                            maximum length 20 characters *)
```

Most UCSD Pascal systems make an absolute upper bound of 255 characters on the lengths of strings.

WRITE and WRITELN

These two procedures differ from the standard Pascal versions in two ways: (1) they do not support printing out Boolean values, and (2) they will print out STRING variables, as described above.

Case Statements

Standard Pascal specifies that if there is no label matching the value of the selector, the result of the CASE statement is undefined. UCSD Pascal defines that, if there is no label matching the value of the CASE statement, the CASE statement is treated as if it were a dummy "no operation" statement, and the next statement following the CASE statement is executed. Thus this is a sort of generalized "otherwise" case for the CASE statement: "Otherwise, do nothing and go on to the next statement."

Interactive Files

The type INTERACTIVE is a predeclared type just like the type TEXT (= file of CHAR) except for manner in which files of this type interact with READ and READLN. If F has been declared to be a TEXT file and CH has been declared to be of type CHAR, Standard Pascal makes READ(F,CH) equivalent to the following two statements:

```
   CH := F^;
   GET(F);
```

This means that when the file is first opened (before the very first READ from it), the file window variable F^ must already be initialized with a value; i.e., that an automatic GET(F) is done when the file is opened. This is fine when F is a disk file. But if F is supposed to be a file associated with a terminal to get input from the user, then right from the beginning, the program is expecting a character to be typed, and it will do nothing until it gets the character. INTERACTIVE files overcome this problem. The type INTERACTIVE behaves just like the type TEXT except that if F has been declared to be of type INTERACTIVE, then READ(F,CH) is equivalent to the two statements:

```
GET(F);
CH := F^;
```

Thus no automatic GET(F) is done when it is opened.

Random Access Files

If FOLDER has been declared to be of some record type and F has been declared to be of type file of FOLDER, the UCSD Pascal system allows essentially random access to the records in the disk file corresponding to F. The system sequentially numbers the records in the file starting with 0. Then the file window F can be positioned at the beginning of the record number k by use of the intrinsic procedure SEEK. This procedure takes two arguments, first the file identifier, and second the number of the desired record. Thus

```
SEEK(F,15)
```

would position the file window F at the 15th record in the file. The file F should be opened with the RESET(F) instruction. After use of SEEK, the given record may be read in via a GET or updated by overwriting it with a PUT. Attempting to SEEK a record beyond the physical end of the file F will cause EOF(F) to become true.

Index